I, The Prophet

I, The Prophet

Dramatic Monologs for Today
from
Twelve Old Testament Prophets

RICHARD BAUERLE

Publishing House
St. Louis

The Scripture quotations in this publication are from the Revised Standard Version of the Bible, copyrighted 1946, 1952, © 1971, 1973 by the Division of Christian Education of the National Council of the Churches of Christ in the U.S.A., and used by permission.

Copyright © 1981
Concordia Publishing House
3558 South Jefferson Avenue
St. Louis, Missouri 63118

Manufactured in the United States of America

1 2 3 4 5 6 7 8 9 10 WP WP 90 89 88 87 86 85 84 83 82 81

Library of Congress Cataloging in Publication Data

Bauerle, Richard E., 1928-
    I, the prophet.

    1. Bible. O.T. Prophets—Sermons. 2. Sermons, English. 3. Lutheran Church—Sermons. 4. Christian drama, American. 5. Monologues. I. Title.
BS1505.4.B38   224'.09505   81-3140
ISBN 0-570-03835-9   AACR2

To Bonnie, whose name identifies her personality

Contents

Preface

The messages in this book were delivered at Zion Lutheran Church, Sandusky, Ohio, over a two-year period during seasons of Lent. Although they may not be traditional Lenten messages, they were well received during this special devotional period of the church year as a supplement to other services in which the Passion and Death of Christ were preached.

My purpose in writing and preaching these sermons in the first person was twofold. First, I am aware that if there is one part of Scripture that is less known than any other, it is the message of the prophets. Yet the message of the prophets is as modern as the daily newspaper and should be heard in our day in special ways.

Second, I preached them in the first person, costume and all, to make them more personal. My hope was that the prophet would become real through my portrayals, and I believe I was successful in this attempt.

I can visualize these characterizations used as a textbook on an introduction to the prophets, or as the basis for a Bible study in a local congregation. My own personal preference, however, is for use as preaching for special occasions and seasons. Amos could make the basis for an Ash Wednesday sermon, and Isaiah for Good Friday or Holy Week; Enoch, Micah, Habakkuk, and Zechariah could be used during Advent; Malachi as a stewardship sermon; and Daniel on a national holiday. Some pastors are using Old Testament series, and I could see them inserted in such a series from time to time. Those to whom I preach seemed to appreciate them during the penitential season of Lent.

The prophets deserve our attention. My prayer is that this small effort on my part will help draw more attention to them.

Richard Bauerle

1
I, Amos

I am the prophet Amos. I often wondered why the Lord chose me to be a prophet. I certainly had not prepared myself for it. I was not trained in one of the schools of prophets like some of the rest of them. Elijah used to have a whole group of young men following him around whom he trained to be prophets. Other prophets also trained others to be prophets, but I was not one of those. My education was limited, to say the least.

I was a herdsman in Tekoa, taking care of my sheep and goats. It was a wild country, full of wild beasts and thorns and brush, and I was like the land—wild and beastly. I had to be so, in order to take care of my flocks. It was my life. It was the only life I knew.

One day, out there in that wild wilderness, the Lord came to me and said: "Amos, I have a burden on My heart that I want you to deliver for Me. I want you to be My prophet to Israel for a short time." You can imagine my surprise. "Why me, Lord," I said. "I am not trained to be a prophet—why, I even stammer when I speak. You have all sorts of prophets down there in Israel who were trained to be prophets. Why don't You get one of those to be Your spokesman?"

The Lord replied to me: "Amos, there is a famine in the land. Not a famine of food, but of the Word of the Lord. Those prophets are not preaching My Word. They are preaching what the people want to hear, and I have a message to give to them, but they won't give it. And besides, those prophets are infected with the same affliction with which the people are afflicted. The prosperity of the land has made even the prophets live only for greed and wealth. There isn't anyone down there in Israel who has not been eaten up by greed! So, Amos, it has to be you. You are the one who must tell them. You have not as yet been touched by that prosperity up here in this wilderness. It has to be you, Amos, who must go."

I must confess, I had not thought about that before. It had not occurred to me what prosperity does to spiritual life. Everyone has greed, but when there is not much prosperity, there are not so many ways for this greed to find expression. But when there is prosperity—when it is there to get—then everyone is going out to get it. They want to be the first to get the most.

The Lord then told me something else that both depressed and angered me. "Amos," He said, "it is already too late. I am not sending you to these rebellious people in order to save them, but only to tell them *why* I have to destroy them. They are not going to listen to you. It is already too late. Their prosperity and greed have already destroyed them." After He told me this, I knew I would have to leave my flocks for a while and preach the burden that the Lord had placed on me.

Does that frighten you? The age in which you are living is exactly like mine. You are witnessing what prosperity can do to the spiritual life of a nation. You have begun to see the decay of your society because of greed. You have begun to see churches, once strong and influential, half empty. You are witnessing a famine in your land of the Word of God when many preachers are preaching everything except the Word of God and telling the people what they want to hear. Does it frighten you to see it happening? Is it already too late for you? It was for us! It was already too late when God called me to be a prophet.

That's why God came to me, a wild, beastly herdsman, to bring His message. It was going to be rough, because they were not going to listen, and they were going to mistreat me and abuse me. But what did I care? I was used to that. I used to fight wild beasts with my bare hands! I would be able to handle whatever circumstances arose.

I felt like Jonah, who was called by God to preach to Nineveh. Jonah didn't want those people to listen to him, because he wanted to see that wicked city destroyed. Those people down there in Israel on their beds of ease and in their luxurious homes didn't bother me. I was used to their contempt. In fact, I rather enjoyed my message of doom to them. I had had enough of their contempt, and now it was my turn! I didn't need them! I didn't have to stay very long among them. My ministry among them only lasted a couple of weeks, and then I went back to my herds. So what did I care what they thought of me? I didn't mind at all the kind of message I was to bring.

Let me tell you what the Lord showed to me, and what I, in turn, delivered to the people of Israel, and see what you think the Lord would show me if I were to be sent to you with His message.

I heard the Lord ROAR out of Zion! His voice poured out of Jerusalem! His voice made the pastures wither and the mountain tops melt. "For three transgressions of Israel," He said, "and for four transgressions, I will not revoke My punishment. They have rejected the law of the Lord; they have not kept My statutes; they have led themselves astray by their own lies; and they kept the prophets from speaking. For those four transgressions, I will never forgive them."

The Lord continued to speak to me, saying: "These people, the children of Israel, are the only people I have ever so blessed. They were My people. I brought them out of bondage, and I made them Mine. I led them for 40 years in the wilderness. I gave them a good land. These, of all the people in the world, are Mine, and I protected them. I wanted for them every good thing, and I wanted them to know what their sin was doing to them. I only wanted them to know two things. First, how much I loved them, and second, what sin could do to them. But they would not listen! They got worse and worse. Not only did they leave Me to go chasing after other gods, but they also began abusing one another in their efforts to gain wealth."

"Those fatted cows of Bashan!" He roared. "They are known for having the finest pastures and the clearest water to drink in all the land. They are the fattest cows, and the sleekest, in all the land, and then they break down their fences to get over into some one else's pasture, where the grass is not nearly as green and the waters not nearly so clean. I am just going to *have* to put hooks in their noses and in their flesh to draw them out like you would draw a fish out of water. They just won't listen! Their greed is insatiable!"

Then the Lord said to me: "I tried in every way to warn them so I wouldn't have to do this, but they would not listen! I kept giving them little warnings. I withheld rain at the end of their harvest so that their crops would bear a little, but not much, so that bread was scarce. But they would not listen to that warning. Then I sent rain to one part of the country and not to the other, so that there was a scarcity of water in one place, and too much in another. But that did not make them return to Me either. Then I made meat scarce, so that they had a little but not much, and only the wealthy could afford it. But they would not listen to My little warnings. I then brought them more powerful warnings. I had little wars break out here and there, not in order to destroy the nation, but that many of their young men would die and the nation would be drained of its resources. But they would not listen even to that!" (Is that beginning to sound familiar to you?)

The Lord continued: "Then I made the nations around them stronger and stronger. They could see that other nations were beginning to overtake them in arms and strength, but even that would not make them return to Me. Finally, I did something I had hoped I would never have to do. I took away from them My Word! I hoped that when they no longer heard My Word, they would become hungry for it. I didn't send any good preachers to them, and those who did preach would not preach My Word, but only things they thought the people wanted to hear. I thought they would get hungry for My Word again when it was taken from them, but they did not! They did not even want My Word!" All these things the Lord said unto me.

As I began my ministry among them, I noticed all this to be true. They did not want to hear God's Word. In fact, they were even complaining that they had to close up their shops on the Sabbath. They wanted to continue their work and business so they would not lose that one day in making money. Their greed had no end! They just would not listen! If you think I am getting this out of your daily newspapers, you are wrong! This you will find written in my Book of the Prophet Amos.

In spite of all the warnings the Lord gave them, they still went down to Bethel where a golden calf was, and they worshiped there. They went up to Beersheba, where all the idols of sex were, and they mingled with the prostitutes, both male and female. The judges took bribes from the rich to take advantage of the poor. The poor had to pay the judges for rights that were already theirs by law. They attacked one another with lies. Businessmen used false weights. Some wanted war for their personal gain. They persecuted the true prophets. There was no end to their abominations, in spite of all the warnings the Lord gave them.

But none of those things infuriated the Lord as much as something else did. Let me tell you what it was. Those people who went whoring after other gods; who lied about their neighbors; who cheated in their business; who wanted war for their own gain; who didn't want to hear the Word of God—those people still came to the Lord's house to offer their sacrifices to the Lord, with their singing and their feasting. The worst abomination of all was when the wicked would come to worship God. They still brought their offerings, and God hated it! They were still holding their feast days in God's honor as if everything was alright, and God despised it! They were still singing their hymns and anthems, and God *loathed* the sound of their music! Here is what the Lord told me to tell them: "I don't want your sacrifices. When I was with you in the wilderness, you did not sacrifice to Me for 40 years, and I did not mind that. What I minded was your murmurings against Me and My servant Moses. I did not miss your sacrifices, but I did miss your trust in Me. Just who do you think you are sacrificing to—to one of your many gods? You sacrifice to other gods all week, and now you bring sacrifices to Me on the Sabbath? Just who do you think you are? Who do you think I am? I hate, I despise your feasts, and I take no delight in your solemn assemblies. Even though you offer Me your burnt offerings and cereal offerings, I will not accept them. I will not look upon the peace offerings of your fatted beasts. But let justice roll down like waters, and righteousness like an everflowing stream. You dare not divide your life from your religion."

When the Lord told me that, I knew that only a complete reform by these people would stop the coming deluge of God's anger. They took God's mercy for granted, and that would not do. Their services of religion would not save them. Their long privilege as members of God's chosen people would not help them. God would not even listen to their prayers. Only *total* reform would save them.

I must confess I became terrified at the sight of what the Lord was about to do to my land. He showed me famine and pestilence and plagues and fires of war. He showed me my land totally destroyed. I was a shepherd, and I remember the day when a lion came into my little flock and grabbed a lamb and ran off with it. I caught that lion and I killed it with my bare hands, but all that was left of my precious lamb was two hind feet and a piece of its ear. The Lord told me that this was all that would be left of Israel—a couple of small broken pieces of flesh that was once a whole body. "The lion is now roaring as it is near the prey," He said.

I tried to stop God from doing it. It was the prophet's job to pray for the people, and I did. For a moment, the Lord hesitated doing what He was about to do because of my prayers, for He wanted me to know again why He had to do what He had to do. After all, He chose me to be a prophet, so He explained it to me again. He said to me: "I will test it again and once more will I go through the land to find some righteous person." But he could find none, and came to me again, saying: "This nation is so ripe it is rotten to the core. They are worse than Sodom and Gomorrah!"

As I stood there in the temple, I was aghast as I watched the Lord rouse Himself! He went to the altar and stood on the altar and would permit no one to bring any more sacrifices. He would not even listen to me. He roared at me and said: "Get out of My way and open up the gates of the temple! Throw them open wide, for I am leaving My house desolate! If anyone tries to stop you, *bash in their heads*! I will not be stopped again! I will smite first the kings and the princes; then I will smite the prophets; then the rest of the people! If they try to hide from Me, I will find them! If they go even to hell, I will pull them out! If they go even to heaven, I will tear them out! If they go to the bottom of the sea, I will have serpents bite them! When they want to save their children, they will rush in to their homes to hide their children there, only to find that the enemy is inside the house! When they run from the lion, they will run right into the claws of the bear! When they stop to rest by the wall, a snake will be on the wall to strike them! No one will escape, for nothing can stop the fury of My wrath!"

That was the burden with which I was entrusted. I was to speak it, and I did. Is it any wonder that my name, "Amos," means "Burden Bearer"? It was a heavy burden to bear.

The high priest, Amaziah, met me one day and told me to get out of Israel. "Don't tell us those things," he said. "You are only disturbing us. You have become a nuisance to us, and we don't want you here in Israel. Why don't you go down to Judah, where they will listen to you?" I told him that Judah does not need me. They have a great king down there, Uzziah, and they have great prophets of their own to whom the people are listening. They need me here, I said. He then tried to have me killed.

I told him: "Amaziah, I am not a priest, and you have no control over me. I am not really a prophet, only a herdsman. I am not a trained preacher, but I must bear the burden that the Lord has

16

given me. And as for you, Amaziah, you are going to be carried away into bondage. Your children will all be killed in the slaughter, and your wife, because there is nothing else she can do to stay alive, will become a harlot—all because you would not listen. You are the one who should have been giving this message to the people. You may have been able to save this people if you would have been faithful, but because you did not do your job, you will suffer for it." And it was so!

Let me say just this to you. Don't think I came without bringing some hope. I told them at the end of my message that a small remnant would return from bondage—just a little remnant—only about 10 percent. But out of that 10 percent the Lord would raise up a man, a stump of David, who would lead the people out of captivity. I wish I could have known Him in my lifetime. But you know Him. He is the Christ, whom you know.

2
I, Hosea

My name is Hosea. I was the first of the prophets after the days of Solomon to write my prophecy so that you could know what it was and how I felt about it. Amos was a prophet the same time as I, but my ministry lasted much longer than his. He just came out of the hills and preached for a couple of weeks and then went back to his herds. I was a prophet for 40 years. Isaiah and Micah began their ministry about the time I died, but they were down there in Judah, to the south, while I was up here in Israel, to the north.

I was in a unique position among the prophets. The other prophets were given great visions, and they had great messages to give, but it was given to me to know the heart of God better than any other prophet in those Old Testament times. God wanted those people to know how He felt about them after they had gone astray, and He chose me to tell them—not just with words, but by what happened to me in life.

When the Lord called me to be a prophet, He called me in this way: He said, "Hosea, go and marry a wife. But she whom you marry must be a harlot—a prostitute." Now, the Lord knew me. He knew how sensitive I was. He knew how difficult this would be for me. But He had to choose someone who would feel as He felt when His own people turned harlot and went after other gods.

So I found this harlot, Gomer. I sincerely loved her, and I married her. When we married, I thought she would give up being a harlot. But she didn't. She became a worse harlot than she was before! As a matter of fact, she bore three children—not to me, but to other men while she was my wife. Her lust for men was greater than their lust for her, for if men would not pay her, she would pay them to come to her! Her lust for men was insatiable!

Why, you ask, did God tell me to marry her, knowing what she was and what she would do to me? Ah, therein lies my ministry to

18

Israel. The Lord wanted them to know how He felt when His bride, Israel, turned harlot. That is what the Lord called it when Israel would run after other gods. It was always called "harlotry," for they were committing adultery with other gods and were turning from their husband, the Lord.

Perhaps if I can give you a little background to my ministry, you will understand better what I mean. When David and Solomon were kings of Israel, all Israel was one nation. Those twelve tribes of Israel were one unit. But when Solomon died, the people were quite relieved, for Solomon had taxed them very heavily. He had expensive tastes and lived in great luxury. We were a small nation, and that took a lot of money from us. Why, he had a thousand wives, and he kept them and their servants in luxury. That cost money, and the people of Israel were quite upset about it.

Besides that, Solomon had a great army, with gorgeous horses and chariots. He made intricate systems of irrigations and copper mines and diamond mines—and he built a magnificent temple in Jerusalem. The people were taxed into poverty. You still talk about the wealth of Solomon, but we paid to make him that wealthy!

Even before Solomon died, Jeroboam led a revolt against Solomon, but when the revolt failed, he fled to Egypt and stayed there until Solomon died. When Solomon died, his son Rehoboam went before the people and told them, "Whereas my father laid upon you a heavy yoke, I will add to your yoke. My father chastised you with whips, but I will chastise you with scorpions." In other words, Rehoboam said he would tax us double what Solomon had. You can imagine what Israel did. They revolted. Jeroboam came back from Egypt, and became king of the 10 northern tribes, which we called Israel, and Rehoboam was king of Judah and Benjamin. After the nation split, Jeroboam did not want the people of the northern kingdom to go down to Jerusalem to worship, so he set up some temples of his own in Israel. He set up golden calves in Samaria, which was his capital; also in Dan, which was the northernmost point of Israel; and also in Bethel, which was the southernmost point of the 10 tribes. So they worshiped there in Israel, but they worshiped the golden calves that were the gods of Egypt. That went so well that Jeroboam set up idols all over Israel to worship Baal.

You can imagine what happened. The people became like the gods they worshiped. Everyone became corrupt, from the least of them to the greatest. They had some pangs of conscience about it for a while, but they thought to themselves that if their king told them to do this, it would be alright for them. It took the responsibility away from them, they thought, and gave it to their king.

The people became more and more corrupt. They worshiped those false gods with greater and greater intensity. Elijah tried to stop the tide, but he had little effect on them, even though he had 3,000 priests of Baal slain in a single day. You can see how many priests of Baal there were, for that hardly put a dent in their Baal worship. You must know how it is, once you get that sort of thing started in a society. It spreads like fire, and there is no stopping it. The people loved worshiping those false gods. It permitted them to do what they pleased. The Lord kept calling this adultery, for they left Him, their husband, and went whoring after other gods. It was national harlotry!

It was into that kind of society that I was born. I was prophet to those 10 tribes up north. There was prosperity all around, and because of the prosperity, much greed. Sexual immorality was widespread and unrestrained. Male and female prostitutes were everywhere. That is why everyone seemed to be having a good time. The only thing they were concerned about was enjoying themselves. It seemed on the surface as if things were alright because there was prosperity everywhere. But signs of decline were beginning to show. The people had such greed that nothing satisfied them. Their appetite for sexual immorality began to corrupt everyone. You see, their gods were gods that they created. They wanted to be immoral, so they created a god that permitted them to be immoral. They wanted to live by greed, so they created a god that made it possible to live that way. I know that you are too sophisticated in the 20th century to make gods like that for yourselves, but can you honestly say what you are doing these days is superior to what my people did?

The Lord told me He tried to heal their wounds, but when He began to cleanse their wounds, the wounds were so deep and so festered that they could not be cleansed. When He tried to cleanse them, the stench of those wounds was so bad He could not bear the smell.

When a nation has a moral problem, the problem is deeper than their morals. If you are going to worship the gods of sex, what

20

can you expect? You have noticed from history that when a nation turns from God, simultaneously, the morals go bad, and the greed of the people is aroused. It is like a wind, I said, wrapped up in wings that just keep churning. No one is ever satisfied. Everyone is restless, panting for more. And the wind and the wings were carrying my nation away.

In all of this, do you know what my job was? It was to convince the children of Israel that God still loved them. Other prophets had other jobs, but this one was mine. God was terribly upset about their sin and idolatry, but He never stopped loving them. That is why He had me marry a harlot whom I loved so dearly. In spite of everything she did to me, I still loved her. And all the time she was out playing the harlot, I was preaching God's message to those people telling them how they were destroying themselves. It was not God who was destroying them, I said. They were destroying themselves.

Although my message was a message of doom, I still tried to convince them that God loved them. I told them how Israel had turned harlot, and how they were going to pay for that, because God loved them too much to permit them to continue that way. I explained to them that corruption only brings corruption. I said to them that he who sows to the wind will reap the whirlwind. But in all of this, the people had gone so far down the road to destruction that I was not able to convince them that they were sealing their own doom.

Then I tried to explain to them how bad their harlotry was. First they began to worship other gods. That was harlotry. Then, when they saw that Egypt and Assyria were getting to be very powerful, they first went to Egypt and made an alliance with her. Then they went to Assyria and made an alliance with her. God had always taken care of them. He had always told them not to make alliances with pagan nations, for those alliances were not of any value. Why should they want to make alliances with those godless nations anyway? They could not help Israel.

You see, instead of going to God, they went to other lovers and made alliances with them. They committed adultery as a nation with Egypt and Assyria, for they left the love of God for the love of those foreigners. Then, when Egypt and Assyria said to Israel: "Why do you come to us when you always went to the Lord," Israel said that the Lord had not taken care of them when they went to Him. They lied! That was whoredom at its worst! They lied that God had not taken care of them! That is why I said to them, "Go to your lovers with whom you have made love and see if they will save you now. Just see what their lust for you was worth!"

Here, then, is what I told them: "Israel, you have committed adultery with the golden calf; you have committed adultery with Baal; you have committed adultery with Egypt; you have committed adultery with Assyria. But all the time you were committing adultery with them, you treated them with contempt after you made love to them. Now that you have become old, they no longer want you, and they will remember only the contempt you showed them after you made love to them. That is why they will ravish you and strip you naked and stand you up before the world in shame. Go to your lovers now and see what they do to you, now that you no longer have any beauty to offer them! While you were young and beautiful, they wanted you because God had so blessed you with beauty and wealth. But you wasted your beauty on other lovers. You kissed the calf! You gave away your wealth in making beautiful idols. So now you have nothing to offer your lovers. See how they treat you now!" I told them this because I knew Egypt and Assyria would ravish their land and take them captive and shame them because Israel had nothing to offer them. But through it all, my job was to convince them that in spite of everything they had done, God still loved them.

That is why I did a very strange thing. I had married my harlot wife, Gomer, many years before. In those years, she had lived with every lover who could afford her. She gave birth to three children not mine. But she was now getting old, and no one wanted her anymore. Since she could no longer live on her income as a harlot, she was to be sold as a slave. She could not take care of herself, and no one was willing to take care of her because she had lost her beauty and youth. Now, all that was left for her was to be sold at a slave auction.

The day she was to be sold, the people of my little town wondered what I was doing down there in the town square where she was to be sold. Everyone there knew who she was and what she had done to me. I had preached for those many years about what would happen to the harlot who had left her husband to go to other lovers.

They thought I was there to prove my point. It, was, they

thought, another opportunity for me to tell them again about the harlotry of Israel. Now my message was pat, complete, and perfect. This is where her harlotry had brought her—into slavery. They were there to hear me speak of it.

The whole town was there. I had earned some fame in those years as prophet. As the slaves were put on the block to be sold, they came and went with their buyers with very little interest. Now the awaited moment was here. Gomer, my harlot wife, was on the block. This was the moment everyone was waiting for. What was I going to say when she was sold? Well, I didn't say anything. I did not preach that day. Instead, I went up to the block and stood there to bid for her. *I bought her back!* After all those years, when no one else wanted her, I bought her back, and she was mine again.

Why? The Lord told me to do it. It was His way of expressing His love for His people. I was to represent God, so I bought her back even though she belonged to me in the first place.

I then quoted some of the things the Lord had said to me about His beloved Israel: "When Israel was a child," He said, "I loved him and called him out of Egypt. I taught them how to walk, and I took them up in My arms and healed them, but they did not know I healed them. I drew them with bands of love, and I set food before them. But they did not know. How can I give them up? How can I cast them off? I will not execute the fierceness of My anger. I will not destroy them, for I am God, and not a man. I will not come in wrath. Therefore," He said, "I will allure her, and speak comfortably to her, My beloved Israel."

That's why I bought back my wife, for the Lord would buy back Israel, at great cost. I bought back my wife at great cost—not only in money, but in humiliation—going before all those people and buying her back when no one else wanted her! Not only that, think of my humiliation in buying her back because she did not want me until no one else wanted her.

It was because of this, I saw into the heart of God like no one had seen before. I could not, of course, know the price God was willing to pay to buy back sinners when He sent His own Son into the world and put Him on the cross to pay that enormous price. I did not know the length to which He would go to buy back sinners who didn't want Him—who belonged to Him in the first place. But I did see into the heart of God better than any man before me, for I saw what sin is and what it does to the heart of God. Until my day, everyone thought sin was just a breaking of God's law. No one dreamed that sin is a personal matter that springs from the heart that hates God. No one knew that sin is taking the love of God and spitting on it. It is saying no to God's love. It is the "spirit of whoredom," as I called it, that tramples love under foot. That is what sin is. It is rejecting the love of God.

That is what makes forgiveness so hard. My, it was hard for me to forgive Gomer! It is not an easy thing for God to forgive because His love has been rejected. It is hard to forgive when you are so hurt. Forgiveness is not like throwing a bone to a dog. It costs something to forgive! A tremendous price has to be paid to forgive. You know better than I ever did the price paid on a cross in Jerusalem just to forgive your sins. I knew better than anyone else before me what sin is.

I understood something else that no one else knew. I discovered how God suffers! No one knows how much God loves the sinner. But when that sinner refuses to respond to that love, then God suffers more than the sinner, for God is God, and His love is deeper than any love the sinner can ever understand. Yet, because He loves that sinner so much, God just stands there helpless when the sinner will not be wooed into loving Him in return. God suffers more deeply than any human being can ever understand about this because God is God and His love is deeper than all the love in the world combined. That is why He said to me, "I am God and not a man." "I cannot let her go."

I understood that better than anyone before me, for I always remember how I felt when Gomer left me. I always wondered if it was me! Could I have done something more to keep her from her spirit of whoredom? I know now there was nothing more I could do except to keep loving her as I watched her go to other lovers.

When I lived with that, I saw again the picture of God, wooing and marrying a little slave girl in Egypt, and bringing her out of bondage—giving her freedom—lavishing His tender love upon her day after day, and then watching her as she went to other lovers and crying out to her: "How can I let you go? How can I cast you off?"

God suffers! I knew God better than any man before me, but you know Him better than I, for you know His Christ who paid the price to buy you back.

3
I, Ezekiel

My name is Ezekiel. I was called one of the great prophets of Israel. Whether I was a great prophet, you will have to decide for yourselves. The fact is, I did not choose to be a prophet. Isaiah, that great prophet, who died about a hundred years before me, had a choice whether he would be a prophet, for the Lord came to him one day and said He had a message to give to the people in Jerusalem, and Isaiah volunteered for the job. I didn't volunteer. If I had known what was in store for me, I would probably have done what Jonah did when the Lord called him to preach to Nineveh—I would have run away in the opposite direction.

One day, the Great Jehovah came to me and said: "Ezekiel, I have chosen you to be a watchman over Israel," and that was that! I was a prophet, and I had no choice. My name means "God will strengthen." Little did I know how much strength from God I would need just to bear the message God would give me.

You see, I was not only to give the message. I was to *be* that message! I was the object lesson of the Lord. The Lord had a message of judgment to speak to the inhabitants of Judah as to how they were to suffer, and my unique job as a prophet was not only to speak that message, but to suffer it right before their eyes. When the Lord called me to be a prophet, He told me that I was to be the sign to the house of Israel. They were to be slaughtered, and whoever was left was to be taken captive into Babylon, and I was to be their sign—the object lesson of their slaughter.

Let me tell you how it happened that I became known as a great prophet, although not by choice. The Holy Land consisted of 12 tribes of Israel. After the death of David and Solomon, those 12 tribes split into the northern and southern kingdoms. The Northern Kingdom had 10 tribes, and was called "Israel." The

Southern Kingdom was the tribes of Judah and Simeon, and was called "Judah."

In the year 721 B.C. the Lord made an end of the Northern Kingdom because they became so terribly wicked, and not even the great prophets whom the Lord sent to them could stem the tide of evil. The Southern Kingdom lasted another 140 years. They had some great kings down there for a while—and some great prophets to whom the people listened. But the Southern Kingdom also became terribly wicked and left the Lord for other gods, so the Lord made an end to them also in the year 586 B.C., when the Chaldeans came down from Babylon under Nebuchadnezzar.

Well, 20 years before Nebuchadnezzar made a complete end to them, he came down to Judah with his armies and took some captives with him to Babylon. He took the choicest young men, among whom was my good friend Daniel. Then, nine years later, in 597 B.C., he came back with his army and took some more of us captive, and I was among these later captives. We were not really slaves, because we had much freedom, and we were given our own land and flocks, but we were still exiles away from home. Nebuchadnezzar just wanted some of us up there to work the land. We Jews were together there in one place, and I was their priest.

My good friend Jeremiah was left in Jerusalem and was called by God to be the prophet there in Judah, while I was called to be the prophet and priest among the exiles in Chaldea. I have already complained about being a prophet in Chaldea among the exiles, but the job Jeremiah was given to do was much harder.

After I had been in Chaldea for five years, I was standing by the river Chebar when suddenly a great wind came out of the north, and a great cloud with fire and lightning were flashing out of it as in a storm. It looked as if it were gleaming bronze! This was in July of 592 B.C.

As I watched in wonder, four living creatures came forth towards me, each having the form of a man, but they were not men. They each had four wings, and as they walked, they did not turn right or left but walked straight ahead. They each had four faces. In the front, their face was the face of a man; to the right their face was the face of a lion; to the left the face of an ox; and in the back, the face of an eagle. Their feet were not human feet, but like calves' feet.

You can imagine my fear as they were walking towards me. Then I saw four wheels, one each by the living creatures. Actually, those four wheels were like wheels within wheels that could move in any direction, although they did not turn. Each wheel was covered with eyes inside and out and around, looking in every direction. Covering this entire scene was a firmament, like a rainbow, shining like crystal, and above the firmament, One seated who looked like a man. When He appeared, the living creatures flattened their wings down on the ground, and they knelt there. *And He spoke to me!*

Of course, I knelt too. Actually, I didn't really kneel. I fell down on my face. What could I do? There wasn't anything else I could do. What would you have done?

Then He spoke to me: "Son of man, stand on your feet, and I will speak to you." I immediately stood, and He said to me: "Son of man, I am sending you to be a prophet to My people. They are a rebellious people, impudent and stubborn. You shall say to them, 'Thus says the Lord.' Whether they hear or refuse to hear—for they are a rebellious people—they will at least know there has been a prophet among them. Do not be afraid of them," He said, "but speak what I tell you to speak. Son of man, hear what I say to you, and be not as that rebellious house to whom I send you."

Out of that terrifying vision, a hand came forth and gave me a scroll with writing on it, both in front and back. As I read the scroll, I discovered it was filled with lamentation and mourning and woe. The voice spoke to me again: "Son of man, eat what is offered to you, and digest it, and then speak it to the house of Israel." I did as I was told. I ate that scroll. It was sweet as honey in my mouth, but when it reached my stomach it was bitter as gall, and I wanted to vomit it up. But I could not, and it burned within me! When the vision left me, I was in a bitter heat, and I sat by the Chebar river among the exiles for seven days, overwhelmed!

After those seven days, the Lord came to me again. It was time for my prophecy to begin, but it was not preaching I was to do. Yet, in a sense, it was. I was to be an object lesson. I was told in my vision to lay a brick on the ground and build a miniature siege work about it with iron and ditches. I was in such a way to prophesy against Jerusalem, for such a siege was to lay them waste. The Lord told me He would put invisible cords upon me so I could not move. I was to lie on my left side for 390 days, without moving, in front of that brick. Then I was allowed to turn over on my right side for 40 days more. Each day was to represent a year. Three hundred and ninety years of exile and punishment for Israel, 40 years for Judah. I was their object lesson. I was to suffer their exile! It was my job as prophet to the exiles. My food for that year and seventy days was to be the barest necessities cooked on human dung! You can readily see what my message was to be. Perhaps they would not listen to me, but at least they knew that the Lord had sent a prophet among them.

That began in July, 592 B.C. Then in September, 591 B.C., the Lord came to me again. You can imagine how many questions I had by now. I had had a lot of time to think, lying there for a year and two months. The exiles with me also had the same questions. Since I was both a prophet and priest, I confronted the Lord with our questions: "Lord," I said, "why must we bear such punishment as this? Why do You pour all the punishment upon us when it was our fathers who sinned?"

We had an old proverb in those days that went like this: "The fathers ate sour grapes, and the children's teeth are set on edge." It was our way of saying that the children had to pay for the sins of their fathers. When I said that to the Lord, He thundered at me! "What do you mean," He said, "by repeating this proverb concerning the land of Israel, that the fathers ate sour grapes and the children's teeth are set on edge? As I live," He said, "this proverb shall no more be used in Israel. Everyone pays for his own sin, for all the souls are Mine, the fathers as well as the children. If a man does what is right, he will live. If he begets a son who is evil, that son will die. His father's righteousness will not save him. Or if the father is wicked, and the son is righteous, the father will die and the son will live. The soul that sins shall die, and the soul that is righteous shall live. The son will not suffer the iniquity of his father, nor the father suffer the iniquity of his son. Each man will be judged according to his own way. Never again will I hear in Israel the proverb, 'The fathers ate sour grapes and the children's teeth are set on edge.'"

I was quite stunned by this outburst of passion from the Lord, but He was not finished yet. He said to me: "Son of man, you say I am not righteous in what I will do to My people. Come with Me, and let Me show you what My people are doing." He then took me, in a vision, to Jerusalem. It was nice to be home again, even if it was only in a vision. It was even more pleasant for me when He took me to the temple where I had been with the other priests as I was being trained for the priesthood. It was so nice to be there again. But my pleasure soon turned to bitterness.

That One, like the Son of Man, whom I had seen in my earlier vision, came to me and took me by a lock of my hair and lifted me above the temple, and He said to me: "Look over there by the north gate and tell Me what you see." I looked, and there I saw outside the north gate the vision again that I had seen earlier of the four living creatures, and the wheels, and the rainbow. I was totally unprepared for that! I understood what had happened even before the Lord told me. "See what they have done," He said. "They have put Me outside My own temple!" It was true! They had expelled the Lord from His own temple! How could it have happened? It soon became clear to me as the Lord took me inside the temple. I was astounded at what I saw there! I saw 25 men in that temple looking to the east and bowing down and worshiping the sun! In God's own temple! I don't know how I could have handled more, but more was shown to me.

That One like the Son of Man said to me: "Come, I will show you yet another abomination worse than these." He took me into the inner temple, where priests were to offer sacrifices to God for the sins of the people. What I saw there was beyond anything I can describe! I loathe even speaking of it. There, in the inner chamber of the temple, where priests were to make intercession for the people—there they had set up images of every kind! Oh, I hate describing it! There were images of reptiles, images of the Egyptian gods, images of the gods of the Syrians, images of old Canaan—all there in the inner chamber of God's temple! And there they were, those priests, worshiping those false gods in wild orgies, with their male and female prostitutes being used right in the inner chamber of God's temple!

I could not believe my eyes! Was the vision a lie? How could it be true? Of course, the Lord would not lie to me. It had to be true! But even that was not as horrible as what I recognized then. I recognized the priest who was leading the orgies. Of all people, it was Jaazaniah who was leading the orgies! I knew him! He was trained with me in the temple to be a priest in the finest traditions of our religion. His father, Shaphan, was the priest who worked with King Josiah to purify Judah of its idol worship, and those two men purified the land of abomination. Now, Shaphan's son was leading this abomination! Not only that. Jaazaniah's brothers were Jeremiah's best friends as he tried to bring Judah back to the Lord. That one man—Jaazaniah—destroyed all the work that every good man in Judah tried to perform. He was the son of a great man. He was the brother of great men. But he himself did more evil and created more evil than the good men could overcome.

Now I knew what the Lord meant when He said that every man shall be judged by his own deeds. A father's righteousness will not save a son who is wicked, and a wicked son shall not destroy a father's righteousness, for each man will stand before God alone for what he himself is. No more did I ever use the proverb: "The father ate sour grapes and the children's teeth are set on edge."

Now I knew I must go back and tell the exiles what I had seen. It was not because of their fathers that they must suffer, but because my generation was so wicked. Yes, the fathers sinned, but the children loved the sins of their fathers, and they were worse than their fathers. They themselves deserved what they got, and could not blame their fathers or God.

It was time now, and I, the prophet Ezekiel, understood why Jerusalem was to be laid waste. But not immediately. Nebuchadnezzar laid up a siege around Jerusalem that was not to end for 1½ years (Jer. 39:1-2). The siege began on January 10, 587 B.C.

But I was not finished with my prophesying—not yet finished. The day the siege of Jerusalem began, the Lord came to me and told me that I must again be an object lesson to the exiles. He wanted me to let them know how He felt about the destruction of Jerusalem, and of His people. That night, my wife was to die of a stroke. My beloved—the delight of my eyes—was to be taken from me in an instant. Oh, my! That night, the Lord said, I was permitted to weep for her alone, but I was not allowed to share that sorrow with anyone. That night I was permitted to throw myself across her body and weep and lament, but when the sun rose in the morning, I was not to weep and lament again. I was not to show that first emotion of my sorrow. I was to bear what the Lord felt when His bride, Jerusalem, had to die. He wept for her in private for a while, but not publicly. He could not share His sorrow with anyone.

Can you see why my prophetic office was bitter to me? I must confess I wanted to give up that office, but I could not. The Lord said to me more than once: "Son of man, I have made you a watchman over Israel, and whenever you hear a word from My mouth, you shall speak it and give them warning from Me. And if I say to the wicked, 'You shall surely die,' and you give him no warning from Me that he shall die, then that man will die in his sin, but his blood will I require at your hand." So I continued to prophesy whatever the Lord told me to say. Bitter or not, I spoke it.

I told them about the two harlots—the one was Israel, the other her sister Judah. But it didn't help. They paid no attention to me. The Lord told me that everyone in exile would come and listen to me because they knew there was a prophet among them. It was true. They would come and sit before me because they knew I was a prophet. But the Lord was also right when He told me that they would listen to me as they would listen to a singer of love songs, for they will listen to what you say, but they will not do it, He said. But at least they knew there was a prophet among them. The Lord never leaves His people without a witness.

I spoke much to them about their restoration, telling them they would come back from captivity. It gave me the chance to talk to them about your Christ when He would restore the kingdom of David in the latter days, never to fail again under that Christ. I told them about the valley of the dry bones when they would be put back together again. But there is one vision I want to share with you.

It was very close to the end of my life, and those who had survived the 1½ years of siege in Jerusalem were with me in Chaldea. I repeated to these new exiles what the Lord had told me, that one day they or their children would return to their beloved land. I told them they would never again worship an idol because they would never want to.

I was able to assure them of that because of the amazing thing the Lord said to me. "These people," He said, "will never again defile My name and make Me ashamed to call them My own in the latter days. These people have defiled My name everywhere. When I gave them My land, they defiled My land. When I sent them into bondage and scattered them over the face of the earth, they defiled My name everywhere they went. But never again will they do that! I will see to it that they will never again do that!! Not because of them, but because of My name. I must protect My name, and therefore I am about to act—not for the house of Israel, but to protect My name on the earth. I will make all the nations of the earth know that I am the Lord God, who is holy, and I will do it through My people. Therefore I will take My people, who are scattered throughout the earth in those latter days, and give them back their land. I will cleanse them and put a new heart and a new spirit within them. I will again make them great, and they will never again suffer disgrace. But let it be known to you that it is not for your sake, but for Mine!"

He continued: "I made promises to you that the whole world knows I made, and I will fulfill My promises even though you defiled My name everywhere you went. I made promises and I will keep them—not because of you, but to protect My name! I have a reputation to uphold on the earth!"

"Here is what I will do to accomplish this," He said. "I will be so good to you that it will shame you, for you will remember how you sinned against Me. I will give you every good thing. I will protect you. I will feed you and clothe you and increase your flocks. I will forgive your sins. I will love you and shower you with gifts until you cannot contain it all, and then I will give you more until you cannot bear it—*until you love Me!* Then My name will be vindicated. But I swear to you, I am not doing it for you—I am doing it to protect My name!" Are you aware that the Lord God Jehovah did that for you in Christ—not for your sake, but for His—to protect His name, which is Love?

That is my prophecy. Are you interested in what happened to me? Let me tell you. When the rest of the exiles came up to Chaldea from Jerusalem, they heard what I had said in my prophecies about them, and do you know what they did? They killed me! My own people killed me! Later they said what a great prophet Ezekiel was, but my own generation killed me. What is it about prophets that people cannot stand? I loved those people. All I wanted to do was serve them. I prayed for them. I pleaded with them. I hated the message I had to give them, and believe me, I would have died for them. But they killed me! What is it about prophets in their own generation that people cannot stand?

4
I, Jeremiah

I am Jeremiah. I was called one of the greatest prophets of Israel's history. Perhaps only Elijah and Isaiah would have ranked above me as great prophets. I was not a great prophet because I was such a great man, but because I lived in very trying times, and I happened to be in the middle of things when the whole world in which I lived fell apart.

I was the leader of a brilliant constellation of prophets who were clustered around Jerusalem just before and during our fall to the Babylonian empire. While I was in Jerusalem prophesying, Ezekiel was up in Chaldea near Babylon prophesying to the earlier captives who were taken into captivity first. At that very time, Daniel was preaching in the very palace of Nebuchadnezzar, who eventually destroyed Jerusalem. Habakkuk and Zephaniah were helping me in Jerusalem. Nahum was prophesying to Assyria about the fall of their capital city Nineveh by the same Nebuchadnezzar. And Obadiah was in Edom, prophesying the end of that kingdom.

All these prophets were living the same time as I. It was a terrible time in the history of the world, and the Lord was raising up prophets everywhere—great prophets—known even today as some of the greatest prophets who ever lived. They were all clustered together in my day because the days were evil, and the prospects for the future were so terrible. In those evil days, the Lord was not without a witness, for there were many of us speaking God's truth, but the princes and the priests and the people would not listen to us.

I don't know why the Lord chose me to be the leader of all these prophets. I was not a brilliant man. He could have selected any number of men to do what I did, but He chose me. When I was just 20 years old, while studying in Jerusalem for the priesthood, the Lord came to me and said: "Jeremiah, before I formed you in the womb of

33

your mother, I knew you. Before you were born, I consecrated you and appointed you to be a prophet to the nations."

I did not want to be a prophet, and I frankly told this to the Lord. "I do not want the job of prophet," I said. "I am only a youth with 10 years more before I could be ordained as a priest, and I do not know how to speak," I told Him. But He said to me, "Don't tell Me you are only a youth, for you will go to whomever I send you, and whatever I command, you *will* speak. But do not be afraid, for I am with you to deliver you." I often thought about that during the 50 years I was a prophet—that He would deliver me—for I did not think He *did* deliver me. I told the Lord more than once: "Lord, you deceived me, and I was deceived"! I did not think He delivered me.

Perhaps if I tell you something about myself you will be able to understand why I would speak to the Lord like that. In the first place, I did not really like my job as prophet. I never really wanted to be a prophet. Oh, when I first became a prophet, I was rather thrilled by it, for the Lord gave me the gift to preach. I was a good preacher, and people gladly came to hear me. Then it began to dawn on me—these people were coming to hear me preach, but they had no intention of changing their lives because of what I said. They were just coming to hear me preach! That is why the very gift that God gave to me began to depress me. That is why I was such a complainer. I complained to the people, and I complained to God, but neither the people nor God seemed to care about my complaints. That is why I became known as the weeping prophet. I was always restless and uneasy. Perhaps I complained too much. I had very few friends, although I wanted friends very badly.

I often wondered why I was the way I was. Was it because of me, or was that the way the Lord made me, so that I would work as hard for my people as I did. I was a driven man, both from within and without, because of the great job to which the Lord had appointed me. Why couldn't I have been, I thought, a man who loved confrontation, like Amos did? Why couldn't I have been a man more secure in my feelings towards myself? Then I could have borne what I was given to bear much better. I often wondered which one was the real Jeremiah? Was I the man I appeared to be to those who heard me preach—secure, bold, loving confrontation, unafraid? Or was I what I thought myself to be—uneasy, sensitive, often afraid, hating confrontation.

But the Lord chose me, an insecure, sensitive man to be with those people when the whole world around us was falling apart. I know the Lord always chooses the right man for the job, but why did it have to be so painful to do a job that I did not even want to do? I was the most sensitive and insecure of all the prophets. But that was what made me work harder than all the rest. For 50 years I worked harder and suffered more than all the rest.

I loved those people to whom I preached, more than they will ever know. I fought for them. I even fought the Lord for them. I struggled with the Lord and wrestled with Him so that He would let these people live. I wept over the thought of one of them dying or being taken captive. If I could only have been the Christ so that I could have died for them! But I was not. I was only a prophet. I could not bear the thought of these, my people, being torn apart, so I wept—I pleaded—I prayed for them—I threatened them—I persuaded—I implored them—I begged for them! Night and day I would not let the Lord alone about this as I clung to Him for my people. As I saw these my people going backwards, away from the Lord, into that holocaust of war and destruction, I cried out: "Woe is me, my mother, that you bore me, a man of strife and contention, both within and without, for I have pleaded with the people, and I have pleaded with the Lord, all to no avail." You see, the Lord gave me all that glory, but He put it into an earthen vessel like me who was so weak, and who could so easily break.

What made it so terrible was that no one else seemed to care! The people were going away from the Lord, the temple worship was decaying, princes were corrupt, and immorality was rampant! The Lord told me that no man slept with his own wife anymore, but with some one else's wife. But when I told those people about the holocaust coming because of their sins, do you know what they did? They made me the laughingstock of the city. I became the butt of their jokes. Even their little children made up funny songs about me and were singing them in their streets. They didn't care!

That was terrible enough. But what crushed me more than this was when I discovered that the Lord had already determined what He would do, and would not relent. It had gone too far, and the Lord had given up on them. It made no difference anymore what the people did, because He had already decided what He would do. He told me to tell them to go ahead and sin. "Go ahead and defile My temple," He said. "Come on in and sin in My temple," He said, "or pray—whatever you like. It makes no difference to Me one way or the other." He had already given up on them! They were no longer His children. They were like the Ethiopians, He said. They were no longer God's children. They could do anything they wanted to do. The Lord had determined what He would do, and I could not change that.

Do you see why I was known as the weeping prophet? I complained to the people, and they didn't listen. I complained to the Lord, and He didn't hear. That is why I thought the Lord deceived me. If He called me to be a prophet, then why couldn't I *be* a prophet to make the people listen, and the Lord hear? Why did He call me to fail?

I alone—I alone had to bear the burden of lost souls. The people didn't care. The Lord had determined what He would do. Only I cared! Finally, I couldn't help myself. I cried out: "My anguish, my anguish! I writhe in pain! Oh, the walls of my heart! My heart is beating wildly! I cannot keep silent, because I hear the sound of the trumpet, the alarm of war. Disaster follows disaster. The whole nation is laid waste, and no one seems to care!"—"Is it nothing to you, all ye who pass by? Look and see if there is any sorrow like My sorrow, which was wrought upon Me which the Lord inflicted on the day of His fierce anger."

Ah, yes, I was the weeping prophet—more sensitive than all the rest of the prophets, which made it the more difficult to see it happen—to live through it with them. I wept because I was unable to do anything about it! I was one of the greatest prophets who ever lived, and I could not do anything about what was happening. One day Jesus asked Peter, "Who do men say that I am?" Peter said, "Some say Elijah, some say Jeremiah—" Yes, I was one of the greatest men who ever lived, but I could not do anything to save these people!

Let me tell you about the years—the many long years I was a prophet in Jerusalem—50 years of it! My story really begins before I was born. When David and Solomon were kings in Israel, we were not really that strong, but the Lord protected us by making all our enemies weak. There were no strong nations in those days, so that made us safe. But when Israel became wicked and immoral and began following after other gods, the Lord made the nations around us strong. First it was Egypt, and we barely survived in those days. Then came Assyria, which conquered most of Egypt, and then took captive the 10 tribes of Israel north of us. Assyria then began attacking us, Judah.

But Judah had a great prophet in those days. Isaiah, the Royal Prophet, managed to get to the king, who was also a great man. King Hezekiah and Isaiah together pleaded with the Lord, and in one night, when Assyria had surrounded Jerusalem—in one night the angel of the Lord killed 185,000 of them. My, what a great prophet and a great king could do in those days with their prayers!

But when King Hezekiah died, his son Manasseh became king. Manasseh!!! We never got over him. He was the greatest abomination we ever knew. He was so evil that whenever a king after him was wicked, it was always said of that king that he was almost as bad as Manasseh. He set up idols everywhere. He even brought them into the temple in Jerusalem. He *made* the nation sin!

Well, Manasseh paid for his apostasy! He was taken into Assyria with hooks in his nose and flesh. While he was there, he repented, and the Lord forgave him. Some time later, he was released from captivity and was permitted to return to Judah as king. He tried very hard to set up reforms to undo what he had done, but it was too late. His late repentance saved him, but it could not save Judah. It was already too far gone! His son Ammon ruled for two years, and he was worse than his father ever was. Then Josiah was born. Josiah was only 8 years old when he began to reign as king of Judah, because Ammon had died very young. Josiah's mother really ruled for him until he came of age, and she was a fine lady. Because of her, great reforms were again made under the name of Josiah, but the abomination of Manasseh was already too deeply ingrained in the people, and while outwardly it seemed as if the people served the Lord, they kept their little idols in their homes and worshiped those idols privately. In the middle of Josiah's reign, the call came to me to be a prophet. While Josiah was alive, there was still hope for the nation, but when he died, I felt so alone as I pleaded for this people. There seemed to be no one left to help me. Isaiah had a great king to work with. I did not. The kings and the princes were now corrupt. They gave me no help.

I became aware of that very early in my ministry, and it was then that I realized to what I was called. I was called to preach to a falling nation, and all I could do was prepare them for what was about to happen. I still pleaded with them, although I knew it would do no good. The only good it would do was to keep reminding them why it was about to happen. At least, they always knew the Lord had sent a prophet among them.

I remember the letters I wrote up there to Babylon, where some captives had already been taken, telling them to build houses and raise families up there because they would be there for some time. I would write to Ezekiel and Daniel up there to tell them that the rest of the nation would soon be there in captivity. I did everything I could to make it known that there was no hope for us.

I did some strange things among the people in Jerusalem. I would wear a new garment one day, and then put it under a rock and let it rot there. Then I would wear it among the people, all rotten and torn—to remind them that this is what would happen to them. One day I took a crock to the city dump and smashed it there. I was trying to remind Judah that the crock represented them. I carried a yoke on my back for days, showing them that they would so be in bondage to Babylon.

I even told them to surrender, for there was no hope for them against the might of Babylon. In this way, I tried to save them from famine and death. That is when I was arrested and thrown into a cistern with mire and slop all the way up to my arm pits. I was there for days! They had a terrible time getting me out of there, but they finally sucked me out of it. I was later beaten and thrown into prison and abused.

I kept wondering about the Lord? Why did He tell me not to be afraid of them, for He said He would protect me against them and no harm would come to me? When I complained to Him about that, He told me three things: "Jeremiah, take your eyes off yourself. Come on, now, has it really been that bad? If you think you have had a terrible time of it, just wait, it will get worse! If you are tired of running from foot soldiers, just think what it will be when you run from horsemen. And if you are falling down in a safe land, how will you fare in the jungle? If you think it is bad now, just wait, it will get worse!"

That was the first thing He said. Then He said: "Jeremiah, what are you complaining about? It is not you they hate, it is Me! I loved these people more than you ever will, and it is Me they have turned against, not you. Jeremiah, I hurt much worse than you do."

The third thing He said to me was this: "I will again save them and bring them back. I will keep a remnant safe, and they will return again with one of the sons of David leading them back." That is the way He answered my complaint. He assured me that although He had determined to destroy our nation, He still cared for us.

One day when I complained to the Lord about the people and about their plight and their unfaithfulness, the Lord told me this great thing on which your New Testament is based: "I will make a new covenant with them, not like the covenant that I made with their fathers when I brought them out of Egypt, My covenant that they broke. But I will make a new covenant with them. This is the covenant that I will make with them in those days, says the Lord. I will put My law within them and I will write it upon their hearts; and I will be their God, and they shall be My people. And no longer shall each man teach his neighbor and each his brother saying, 'Know the Lord,' for they shall all know Me, from the least of them to the greatest, for I will forgive their iniquity, and I will remember their sin no more."

Do you know that this is the covenant He made with you when He sent His Son into the world, and then sent His Spirit into your hearts to make you believe and love Him? "I will forgive their iniquity, and I will remember their sins no more" is the promise He has made to you.

Well, Nebuchadnezzar came down from the north and laid a siege around Jerusalem that did not end for 1½ years. In my agony, I stayed all those months in Jerusalem while the siege continued. I suffered everything my people suffered. We all suffered unbearable hardships. We died in the streets; we died in our homes; we died in our palaces. We died of hunger and thirst and malnutrition. I even saw people killing and eating their own children for food. In those months I was not even allowed to pray for these people. The Lord forbad me to pray for them.

After the city fell, Nebuchadnezzar permitted me to stay in Jerusalem because he had heard that I had told the inhabitants of the city to surrender. After the captives were gone, I remember sitting there on a hill outside Jerusalem—sitting there on the same hill where Jesus was crucified some 600 years later. I remember weeping there and saying: "How lonely sits the city that was full of people. How like a widow she has become—she who was great among the nations. She that was a princess among the cities has become a haunt of jackals. She weeps bitterly in the night, with

39

tears on her cheeks. Among all her lovers, she has none to comfort her. All her friends have dealt treacherously with her, and they have become her enemies. Judah has gone into exile because of her affliction, and all the roads to Zion mourn for no one comes to her again, and she dwells now among the nations and finds no resting place. All Jerusalem can do in the days of her affliction and bitterness is to remember all the precious things that were once hers from days of old." Then I thought: "The joy of our hearts has ceased. Our dancing has turned to mourning. The crown has fallen from our heads. Woe to us, for we have sinned."

I sat there long, lamenting my beloved Zion. But it was time for me to go back into the devastated city. A few exiles were left there with me. Now, I want to tell you—all I ever wanted was to be allowed to stay in Jerusalem. That didn't seem like too much to ask after having served as a prophet for 50 years. But those few exiles came to me and grasped me, and dragged me to Egypt with them. There I died. Do you know how I died? My own people stoned me!

I often wondered why the Lord told me: "Do not be afraid of them, for I will protect you from harm." I know now, but I certainly did not understand then.

5
I, Daniel

I am Daniel. By now you must know that each prophet was unique. When the Lord chose someone to be a prophet, He chose him to be a unique prophet. Each was different from the other, both in personality and message. Although all of us prophets had much the same message and the same God, we were all different.

When you speak of me, Daniel, you are speaking of a prophet set aside from all the rest. I was the wisest of all the prophets. As a matter of fact, when Ezekiel was condemning the king of Tyre, that king said something to Ezekiel that he thought was very wise, and Ezekiel said: "What, you are wiser than Daniel?"

But what made me even more different from the rest was that I was raised—and lived—in absolute, ultimate luxury. No man in history lived amidst luxury for as long as I did, not even Solomon in all his glory. It was not by choice that such luxury was mine, but there I was.

When I was a very young man—just a lad—Babylon of Chaldea sent an army to Jerusalem, where I was living. Nebuchadnezzar led that army and took over my city. This was 20 years before the great siege when Nebuchadnezzar came back and destroyed Jerusalem. The first time he came, he took with him the finest young boys of our land to train them to be Chaldeans. The most handsome, the wisest, and the most noble of birth were taken. Four of us who were princes of Judah were taken. These four, all related to the king, of the lineage of David, were brought right to the palace of Nebuchadnezzar and put under strict training. We four, Shadrach, Meshach, Abednego, and I, became the most famous of all those young men. We were not at all to be slaves, but we were to be trained in the ways of Babylon so that we would one day be leaders of Chaldea. There we lived in the most luxurious palace ever built. In fact, while I was there, Nebuchadnezzar built the hanging gardens of Babylon—one of the seven wonders of the ancient world. Nothing else like it has ever been built.

Nebuchadnezzar was the greatest king and conqueror who ever lived. No one has ever surpassed him. Babylon, you know, was the cradle of civilization. This is where they tried to build the tower of Babel. That is why it became known as Babylon. From that time on it was known as the seat of power and glory and of civilization. Hammurabi lived there, and set up a code of laws long before Moses. Some think Moses copied the Ten Commandments from Hammurabi's Code. At the time of Abraham, Babylon was the one world power. Begun by one of Noah's sons, supposedly built in the location of the Garden of Eden, and the favorite residence of the great kings of the ancient world, Babylon the Great was the most magnificent city ever erected. It's walls were 60 miles around, 300 feet high, and 80 feet thick. The whole city was protected by moats around the wall, with 250 towers on the wall, with 100 gates of brass, and drawbridges to each gate that were drawn up every night.

Babylon was the most magnificent, protected city of all time. The palace was the most beautiful ever built—it was even "air conditioned"! There was in that city the greatest wealth ever gathered together in one place. It boasted the greatest king, Nebuchadnezzar. That is where I lived—in the very palace of that great king—as Nebuchadnezzar's favorite.

Can you see what my problem was? I was born of noble blood in Jerusalem. I was taken from my homeland while just a lad. And while my people lived for 20 years in fear, later in poverty, and finally in captivity, I lived in luxury beyond description.

Some of my Jewish descendants have insisted that I should not be called a prophet of Israel. They said I did not suffer as the rest of them did. That was supposed to be one of the marks of a prophet—that he suffered. But what was I to do? It was my place in history, and I had to be a prophet where I was called to be a prophet. The Spirit blows where it wills, and no one knows the coming thereof or the going thereof. I was in Babylon when the Spirit came to me. They say I did not live in Israel when I prophesied. But, of course, that would eliminate Ezekiel too, for he too lived in Chaldea when he prophesied. I suspect that my Jewish descendants are upset about my not suffering, because they were the ones who always caused the prophets to suffer, and they resent me because I deprived them of this.

Of course, the other reason my Jewish descendants do not like my prophecies is that my prophecies were specific as to the time when the Christ was to be born. I had the greatest visions of all the prophets—not *about* the Messiah (as did Isaiah) but as to the *time* when He would be born. I was so specific about the time when the Messiah would be born that it had to be when Rome ruled the world, and it had to be the man Jesus. You can readily see why the Jews do not like my book. They are still waiting for the Christ to be born.

You can understand my problem, can't you? I had to find a way to remain faithful to the God of my fathers while still serving Nebuchadnezzar in that luxurious, magnificent palace. I knew how easy it was to forget God in a situation like that, so I had to be very careful about my life—more careful than anyone else of my generation.

There were, therefore, two things that I did to keep from forgetting the living God while there serving Nebuchadnezzar. I did those two things at great cost to me because I was very high in the court of the king, and everyone wanted to bring me low. I had much to lose by being faithful to God. The first thing I did was that I prayed! I prayed much. That is how I kept my prosperity and luxury from devouring me. I prayed! Three times a day, whatever I was doing, I would stop and go to my window, which faced east towards Jerusalem, and I would pray.

I had so many things for which to pray. I had to pray that in my eminent position I would be kept from pride. I was envied by everyone around me, and I had to pray to be kept from their snares as they tried to pull me down. I had to pray that I would not become dishonest like other eastern rulers. I had to pray for my people in Judah and for those who were taken captive. I pleaded that my people be allowed to return from their bondage in Babylon. If you would have listened at the keyhole of my closet, you would have heard some mighty prayers go before the throne of grace.

Why shouldn't I pray? God had been so good to me. He had treated me with greater favor than anyone else of my generation. Was I to live on the bounty of God and not give thanks for it? God had done so much for me, and I would have robbed God had I not thanked Him.

It was that very thing that gave my enemies a chance to trap me. Everyone knew I prayed to my God three times every day— and more. But I will refer to that later. That is what brought me to the second thing I had to do. I was very careful how I acted when trials beset me. I did not dare bend or compromise my beliefs!

But before I tell you about that, let me explain to you how I came to be one of the rulers of Babylon. I was second only to Nebuchadnezzar in the whole world when he ruled the world. Then when his son Belshazzar ruled with him, I was third in the world in authority. Let me tell you how it happened.

When I was still a young man, having been in Babylon only three years, Nebuchadnezzar had a dream. He was very concerned about it, because he knew it had something to do with his kingdom. No one could interpret the dream for him, so he ordered all his advisors killed. The news reached me, and, young as I was, I asked to see him. When I was brought before him, I first of all told him what the dream was, and then I interpreted it for him. He knew that what I told him was true, because it spoke of his greatness, and he liked that!

That is why he made me his chief counselor. It even pleased him when I asked that the other advisors whom he had condemned to die be permitted to live. I said to him, "They are not able to interpret your dreams, for only God can reveal them." Of course, the other counselors were happy to work under me after I had saved their lives. I held that position for all the years that Nebuchadnezzar ruled the world. During those years, I had several great visions about his kingdom and what would happen to it, and about the kingdoms that would follow his. Then, when his son Belshazzar was old enough, he and Nebuchadnezzar ruled together for a few years, but Belshazzar was good for nothing! All he was concerned about was having a good time. The parties he threw were the most important things he ever did.

My visions told me that the Persians were becoming very strong and would one day take over Babylon. One night it was about to happen. While Belshazzar was having one of his drunken parties, some handwriting appeared on a wall. No one could interpret it, so I was called. As I walked to the banquet hall, I noticed the kind of party it was. It angered me that these great people had now come to the point where they made fun of everything. Nothing was sacred to them. Babylon now resembled Israel before its captivity. When Nebuchadnezzar was king, he knew what made a nation strong, but Belshazzar had lost all discipline. Why, when I arrived at the party to interpret the handwriting on the wall, they were using the sacred vessels from Solomon's temple to drink wine from.

Strange, isn't it? In Jerusalem before their fall, the priests had set up false gods, many of them from Babylon, to defile God's name. Now, in Babylon, they were using the sacred vessels of God's temple to defile the Lord's possessions. That sort of thing always happens before a nation falls.

The handwriting on the wall was clear. It said: "Belshazzar, you have been weighed in the balances, and have been found wanting." That very night the Persians scaled the walls of Babylon, and that great city fell. Now, Darius, king of Persia, ruled the world, and I became his advisor. After him, his son, Cyrus, made me his counselor.

I was a prophet for 70 years! I was a prophet in Babylon for 20 years before Jerusalem fell. I was a prophet during the entire 70 years of their captivity, first under Babylon, and then under Persia. I was still in Persia when the Jews went back to rebuild their city. Who could have asked for more? I chummed about with the greatest men in the world. I was centrally involved in world events of the highest magnitude. Besides, the Lord showed me things about world events, and even more about the Messiah's coming, that He never showed to another man.

But let me tell you something. I did not get there through compromise or politics. I was always true to my God, no matter what. I would *not* compromise, nor would I bend. But that is why I was so trusted.

Let me tell you of one such incident. After Darius had conquered Babylon, he established me as the president of the land of Babylon. There were only three such presidents in the world of Darius. When it was discovered that Darius approved of me more than anyone else, the other rulers and advisors became very envious of me. After all, I was a conquered Jew. What was I doing there? They wondered how Darius could approve of me more than of them.

Those advisors knew something about me that Darius did not

know. They knew that I prayed to God three times a day. Even that late in my life, I would not forget the God of my fathers. That gave them the opportunity to conspire against me. They cleverly conceived of this plan: They went to Darius to have him sign an edict that no one was allowed to pray to any god except Darius for 30 days. They knew me! They knew I would not give up my prayers for a single day. Darius was not aware why they wanted this edict signed, so, in innocence, he signed it. It was one of those edicts which, when once signed, could not be revoked, even by Darius. There was never any doubt in my mind why the edict was made, and there was also never any doubt in my mind as to what I would do.

I ignored the edict. It was never really a problem to me. I was going to be faithful to God, whatever the consequences! After what God had done for me, how could I not pray to Him every day? I could have done as some told me to do. "Daniel," they said, "you must be prudent. You are needed here, and your people, the Jews, need you in high places. You can do more if you don't pray for a month." Or "Daniel," they said, "why don't you pray in secret, so no one will know? After all, you have so much to lose." It would have been so simple for me to do that. There was no doubt in my mind that my God would have accepted my secret prayers as well as my public ones. But, don't you see, the edict was public! So I was going to make a public display of my faith! It would probably have been acceptable to my God had I prayed only in secret, but it was not acceptable to me! It was *my* conscience here, and because the Lord had dealt so graciously with me all my days—and He dealt that way with me publicly—I would not hide in secret, but I would declare my faith in Him publicly!

Besides, it was now my turn! Fifty years before this happened to me, my three friends, Shadrach, Meshach, and Abednego, were put into a fiery furnace because they would not bow down to an image of Nebuchadnezzar. Now it was my turn! I remember how they said to the king, "We will go into the fiery furnace before we bow to that image, and whether our God will save us or not is up to Him, but we say to you, O king, our God *can* save us if He wants to." They were thrown into the fiery furnace, and the furnace was made so hot that the men who threw them into the furnace were burned to death from the heat, but my friends walked around that fiery furnace all night with an angel of the Lord, and they came out of it in the morning without a hair burned. That happened the very year Jerusalem fell to the siege of Nebuchadnezzar. The Lord was still performing miracles and telling us that although Jerusalem fell, He was still Lord. Now it was my turn!

When that edict was signed by Darius, I *immediately* went to my room at the appointed time for my prayers, I opened my window to the east, and I prayed to my God. My enemies waited for me to do that. They arrested me, and threw me into prison. I was to be thrown to the lions in the morning.

King Darius was terribly upset. He didn't know what he had done. He tried very hard to keep me from going to that lions' den, but even the great King Darius could do nothing. When I went into the lions' den, he told me: "May your God, whom you continually serve, deliver you." He even prayed for me all night. In the morning, when he saw me there among the lions, walking about, he said, "O Daniel, has your God even been able to deliver you from the lions?" Of course, my God had! When I walked out of that den, King Darius sentenced the men who had conspired against me to be thrown into the lions' den along with their entire families. I then prospered with King Darius and his son Cyrus all the rest of the days of my life. Didn't the Lord give me a great life?

I wish I could tell you what I saw in my visions. I saw kingdoms come and go as no other prophet. I saw the visions of the Babylonian empire; the Persian empire; the Grecian empire; and finally the Roman empire. I saw the vision of the Christ rise out of that Roman empire. I saw also terrible things, when that Ancient of Days seemed to have been conquered, and I saw Him conquer again. I saw so much concerning the future. I trembled when I saw it. That is why I prayed: "O my God, incline Thine ear to hear; open Thine eyes and behold our desolations and the city that is called by Thy name. We do not present our supplications before Thee on the ground of our righteousness, but on the ground of Thy great mercy. O Lord, hear; O Lord, forgive; O Lord, give heed and act. Delay not, for Thine own sake, O my God, because Thy people are called by Thy name."

6
I, Enoch

I am Enoch. Do you know me? I don't suppose you know very much about me. I am mentioned only three times in the Bible, and then only in a kind of passing reference. But I do not mind. Most of history records only the records of the wicked men. Had I done some wicked deed, I would probably have been mentioned often. But I was not one of those.

History says only of me that I walked with God. That doesn't make much news, does it? But I don't mind. Happy is the man or nation that has made little history, for history records very little that is not evil or filled with wars and revolutions and murder. But a man or nation that has been happy and peaceful and content has no chronicle to attract much attention. I was one of those who were happy and peaceful and content. I was satisfied to walk with God, so not much is said of me.

That, however, does not mean that I did not lead an exciting life. I lived perhaps the most exciting life that has ever been lived on this earth, aside from the life lived here by the Son of God Himself. From those three small references made to me in the Scriptures, you know how exciting my life was.

I lived right in the middle of the period when Adam was made and when Noah was born. In fact, I knew Adam my ancestor, for he lived 317 years after I was born, and Noah was born just 29 years after I left this earth. You see, we lived a long time in those days. Most of us lived over 900 years, so we had many living ancestors. Can you imagine what it was like living in those days? People lived to be nearly 1,000 years old in those days. My son Methuselah lived to be 969 years old! When we would get together for our reunions, we really had reunions! When we talked about the old days, we talked about the *old* days!

I remember how I used to sit on old Grampa Adam's lap. I was the seventh generation after him, but I called him Grampa because he was the oldest. I never tired of hearing him tell about the days he and Eve lived in the Garden of Eden. He would talk about the green grass, and the blue waters, and about the trees. I would listen intently as he would talk about the fact that there were no thorns or thistles or pain or tears or sorrow or hunger or death. He always had a faraway look when he spoke of the peace and love between himself and Eve and the rest of the creatures.

Whenever I would see Adam, I kept asking him to tell me again the story of the Garden of Eden, where he and Eve lived, but he didn't like to talk about it very much. It always pained him to talk about it to me, for he knew that I would always ask him: "But, Grampa, why can't we live in that garden again?" It was painful for him to tell me what he and Eve had done. They had deliberately done what the Lord told them not to do, so the Lord would not permit them to live in Paradise again.

I will always remember the way he looked when he told me that. When he would begin telling me about the Garden, I could see his eyes light up at the thought of the things they did there. But as he would talk a while, his eyes would grow sad and he would just shake his head as he looked at me in such anguish as he told me that we could not go back there until we died. I know he looked at me that way because he felt responsible for the fact that I would never see that garden or live in it until I died.

It wasn't so bad for me, because I had never been there. I could only imagine what it was like from what Adam told me. But Adam had been there! He knew what Paradise was, and he knew what life was like *outside* of Paradise, and he knew from what he had fallen. He knew also what he had caused within the human race, for, because of his sin, the race of men would know sin and shame and sorrow and pain and tears and death.

When I became older and could begin to understand the agony that Adam felt every time he talked about the Garden, I didn't ask him about it anymore. It did not seem to satisfy him that the Lord had promised Eve a seed that would one day bring them to paradise in heaven. They thought Cain was that seed, but that too was a disappointment. I always wondered why I couldn't live in a paradise here on earth. Why did I have to die to find it?

Adam used to tell me how he and Eve would walk in the Garden in the cool of the evening and wait for God to come and walk with them. What a delight it was for them! That was what made Paradise what it was—that they walked and talked with God in the cool of the evening. But then, when they sinned, they hid themselves from God because they were ashamed and afraid of God. They didn't want to walk with Him anymore. For all intents and purposes, Paradise was already gone for them, even before God would not permit them in the Garden anymore. Their Paradise was ended when they no longer walked with God.

As I thought of that, I began to wonder—why couldn't I get Paradise back on earth if I found a way to walk with God again? If I could walk with God again, would it be possible for me to get back at least a vestige of Paradise on earth? It was true! It was possible! I found a way to walk with God, and a huge portion of Paradise was returned to me on earth. Then, when I was 365 years old, I walked with God right into heaven—right into total and everlasting paradise.

I wonder why anyone would want it any other way. If it is possible to walk with God on earth, why don't more people do it? In my own age, I was the only one. Oh, perhaps Adam's second son, Abel, would have done it, for he knew God well, but he didn't live very long, you know. Cain got jealous of him one day and killed him. That was the first death that ever occurred on earth. I can just see Cain standing over Abel with a club in his hand, wondering what had happened. He had never seen death before. He had only heard that the wages of sin is death. It is appropriate that death should have come for the first time on our planet in a violent way when a brother killed a brother.

If you think it was easier in my day to walk with God than it is in yours, you are wrong! My day was like yours. It was a day when judgment was on its way, just as it appears to be in yours. I was only one generation away from the flood of Noah's day when the Lord nearly made a complete end of mankind because we were so evil. When Jude, in your New Testament, writes of me, he speaks of the wickedness of man and how God warns the wicked of the impending judgment. He said: "It was of these also . . . that Enoch prophesied, saying, 'Behold, the Lord came with His holy myriads, to execute judgment on all, and to convict all the ungodly of all their deeds of ungodliness that they have committed in such an ungodly way, and of all the harsh things that ungodly sinners have spoken against Him.' These are the grumblers, malcontents following their own passions, loud-mouthed boasters, flattering people to gain advantage" (vv. 14-16).

That is what it was like in my day. The judgment was coming because the people were no longer following God, but did everything in an ungodly way. I, in my day, spoke against it. That is the reason why I could be numbered among the prophets of old. I was also a prophet in my day.

Since I was one of the few in my day who spoke against the evils, I bore the brunt of all their anger and sin. I *had* to walk with God, or I could not have borne it. They were evil days. I was living at the close of an era of mankind when the Lord had had enough and decided to make an end to it. I lived just before the great flood, when my great-grandson walked into an ark with his children and all those animals. The people in my day were grumblers, complainers, following after their sexual lusts, loud-mouthed boasters, everyone trying to take advantage of another, just like Jude said.

We had a problem in my day that you don't have. People lived long, and the older they became, the more wicked they were! You would think that as they grew older, they would not *want* to be so wicked, for as they grew older, they needed so much less from other people, for they could build up their wealth over all those years. They didn't need more, but they were never satisfied. They grew more wicked with age!

Your poet Wordsworth said that when a child comes into the world, he has some memory of heaven. That is why it is so easy for him to believe. Then, he said, as the child grows older, the years slowly take that vision from him and it does not return to him until his old age. Well, the vision of Paradise was very close to us in my day. It wasn't that long before, when Grampa Adam lived in the Garden of Eden. But the longer we lived away from the vision of that Garden, the more wicked we became. Perhaps when my generation lived to be 900 years old, we began thinking of God and Paradise again, but in the meantime, when we forgot that vision, it was a long, long time from infancy to 900 years. Yes, in order to keep men from becoming so wicked, God had to shorten our years for our own good.

Let me tell you how it was that I walked with God. The writer to the Hebrews says that I walked with God *in faith*. I trusted God, so I walked with him all the way. Why should I go in another direction, when I trusted God? You see, I did not walk in front of Him, I did not walk behind Him, I walked *with* Him. Step by step, I walked with God and He with me. It seems very strange to me that anyone would have *wanted* to walk away from God when He is so trustworthy and lovely. It was so nice to walk with God. I was always safe and secure. I was always happy and content because I trusted God.

I knew there was nothing He could not handle. When those people railed against me, and abused me, and attacked me, I was not concerned, because I walked with God and He was totally trustworthy. He was master of every situation, and there I was, walking beside Him, totally safe and secure. How nice that was! I don't know why anyone would want it any other way. Why, it was almost like being in the Garden of Eden.

I thought to myself what a great advantage that was to me, to walk with God and be sheltered in His everlasting arms. It *was* an advantage to me. But what I did not understand at first, but later learned, was that this is the way God wanted it too! I not only walked with God, He walked with me! He walked with me because He wanted to. He liked it too! In fact, God liked it so much that one day while I was walking with Him, He began walking faster and faster, and as I was trying to keep up with Him, I suddenly realized I had walked with Him right into heaven. I reached His home much sooner than I ever thought I would. I was comparatively young at the time—only 365 years old—only about half of the lifetime of my relatives. It was only about noon in my life when the Lord said to me: "Enoch, come on home. There is no need for you to be out of heaven any longer. You have lived your life. You have walked with me in that imperfect world long enough. Now, come on home." And, young as I was, it was nice to be home.

My friends and relatives looked for me everywhere but could not find me. I had gone home. What a privilege! To be allowed to walk with God all the days of my life, and to have vestiges of Paradise all my earthly days, and then to go home to complete and everlasting paradise is the greatest privilege anyone can have.

Now, you say to me that that was alright for me, but no one could ever do it now. Why not? You know more about God than I ever did. You know the love of God. You know that whether or not you want to walk with Him, He wants to walk with you. You *must* know this is the reason He sent His Son into the world to walk those dusty roads of Palestine. Your God even died and went to a grave to let you know He wants to walk with you forever. He sent His Spirit into your hearts to be with you always. Why can't you walk with Him now? God did all this to tell you He wants to walk with you. Believe in Him, and you will *want* to walk with Him, and you will walk together.

Think of it! It would be great for you to walk with the President. It would be an honor for you to walk with the Queen of England. But think what it is like to walk with the Creator of the universe, the Giver of health and wealth and life, the Maker of the sea and the land and the sky. Think of the honor to walk with Him all the days of your life. He wants to walk with you. He wouldn't have come into this world to die if He would not have wanted it desperately. You can walk with Him like I did if you believe.

Let me mention just one more thing. I was taken to heaven *bodily*. It was in the body that I went to heaven. They searched for my body, but they could not find it. Someone would say, "Where is Enoch?" Someone else would say, "God took him." Then someone else would say, "Well, where is his body?" You see, Abel was already dead. Adam was also dead, and they knew that their bodies stayed on earth. But my body was in heaven with me. Can you see what testimony this is! The body is capable of immortality! Not just the soul, but the body has the capacity to live forever! You believe in the resurrection of the body. The body is capable of living forever! On the day of resurrection, you will be given back your bodies. Oh, not one like you have now, but you will be recognized in your body. That is the testimony of the Very Son of God. These bodies of yours will be given back to you when Christ returns to judge the earth. That is the testimony of Christ, and you celebrate that over and over again, each time you come together to worship. This is my testimony to you—your body has the capacity to live forever.

Isn't that nice! You are allowed to walk with God in this life in the body, then you will walk with God for a while in heaven without your body, and then you will get back a renewed body on the day of resurrection. Then you will walk with God forever in your body. Isn't that nice. Be like me! Walk with God!

7
I, Isaiah

I am the Royal Prophet, Isaiah. I am so named because I was of royal blood. Uzziah, that great King of Judah, was my cousin. His father, Amaziah, and my father Amos were brothers. Does it seem strange to you that a man of royal blood, who perhaps could have been a king of Judah, would be a prophet? Could one raised in a palace be a good prophet? One accustomed to wealth and luxury—could he be a good spokesman for God?

What difference does it make who one is, or what his background is? He can be a prophet if he is called to be a prophet! For that matter, I was the only prophet to volunteer for the job. Most of the rest of them tried to avoid the position. I volunteered. Perhaps that is the reason I had such great visions of the Christ—visions that no other man ever had. In fact, I saw the Lord more than any other man who had ever lived until He was born. Oh, I had visions about our nation like the other prophets did. I saw the end of our nation too, just like the others, but I am known for my visions of the Lord when He would walk the earth.

I saw so many visions of the Christ that many of your modern commentators insist that much of my book was written after the time of the Christ. They say that no none could have seen what I saw of the Christ unless I was there in person to see it. Those commentators received quite a shock, when in 1947, a scroll was found that had been put into a pottery vessel filled with pitch. That scroll, found near the Dead Sea, contained my entire prophecy. That scroll, nearly 24 feet long, was written before the time of Christ. Ah, yes, I saw it all before it happened. That must be of great comfort to you. It assures you that it was the Lord who showed me all that, and it assures you that the Christ whom you worship is the Savior of the world.

I am anxious to tell you my story. When my cousin, King

Uzziah, was king in Judah, he was a great king. But one day he became very proud of his successes and took credit for things that the Lord had done for him. He went into the temple in that weak moment and stretched forth his hand and did what only a priest was allowed to do. The Lord had always assigned jobs to different people, and each was to do his own job. The king was to be king, and the priest was to be priest, and neither was to interfere with the job of the other. For this reason He gives gifts to people to do their own work. But to each his own. My cousin, Uzziah, was given great success as king, but he became proud—so proud, in fact, that he thought he had a right to function also as a priest. He felt, because of the successes that the Lord had given to him, that he had earned the right to take unto himself the task of doing sacred things that the priests alone were consecrated to do.

While he was in the temple performing priestly duties, he was struck with leprosy. Shortly after that he died. I had a difficult time with that, and I thought my world had ended. Uzziah was not only my cousin, but he was my good friend. After he died, I went into the temple, not to carry on the priestly functions, but to pray. While I was there, I saw the Lord for the first time.

I saw the Lord, high and lifted up, and His train filled the temple. Above Him stood the seraphim, each having six wings. With two wings they covered their face, with two wings they covered their feet, and with two wings they flew. One called to another and said, "Holy, holy, holy is the Lord of hosts, the whole earth is full of His glory!" The foundations of the threshold shook at the voice of him who called, and the house was filled with smoke.

You can imagine how I felt! I felt as if I would die! I felt unclean, and that the people with whom I lived were unclean. I thought that I would surely die!

Then one of the seraphim took a tongs and went up to the altar in the temple and took a piece of burning coal from the altar, and he touched my lips with it and said to me: "Your lips are clean." Then He who sat on the throne said: "I have a message to give to the people. Whom shall I send?" I said, "Here am I, send me." I volunteered!

It is strange how my life changed from that moment. Before this time, I would look around and see things going bad, and I would say to myself, "Why doesn't someone do something about it?" Now I realized that it was my responsibility to try to do something myself. Now it was not someone else—it was *I* to whom the responsibility was given. Everything was so different now.

I will never forget how I felt when I saw the Lord the first time. How unclean I felt! How unworthy! But how clean I felt when the Lord told me I was clean! I never forgot that. All those visions I saw of the Christ made me feel the same way.

You may not be aware of the fact that so many of the visions that I had of the Christ were inserted into other visions about my nation and world events. It was as if the Lord was saying that when the Messiah comes, He will come right in the middle of great world events, and that He would deal with the problems of the world right in the middle of the common events of mankind.

There was that day, for instance, when my king, King Ahaz, had lost heart. Syria was attacking Judah and they joined forces with Israel to the north of us. King Ahaz could not see how we could ever survive those enemies together. I said to him, "Don't worry, the Lord will save us," but he could not believe me. So I said to him, "I will show you a sign. The Lord will show you any sign you wish—just name it and the Lord will show that sign to prove to you that Syria and Israel will not conquer you." But he was shy and did not want the Lord to show him a sign. I said to him again, "The Lord has said He will give you any sign you wish, even if it is as deep as hell." But he did not want to put the Lord to the test. So I said to him that the Lord would give him a sign anyway. "Behold," I said, "a virgin will conceive and bear a Son, and will call His name Immanuel, which means 'God with us.'" And there Christ was introduced.

Another time the Lord told me what would happen to these rebellious people. These people of Mine, He said, are terribly rebellious. Do not be like them! They are unfaithful! They are going to false gods everywhere! They are consulting mediums and witches, they are consulting false prophets, but they do not call upon Me. For that reason, He told me, they would look everywhere for help when destruction comes to them, but they will not be able to find it. They will turn their faces upward and from side to side on earth, but behold, all will be darkness to them. Then He said this great thing to me: "The people who walked in darkness have seen a great light.... For to us a Child is born, to us a Son is given; and the government will be upon His shoulder, and His name will be called Wonderful Counselor, Mighty God, Everlasting Father, Prince of Peace. Of the increase of His government and of peace there will be no end, upon the throne of David, and over His kingdom, to establish it and to uphold it with justice and with righteousness from this time forth and forevermore. The zeal of the Lord of hosts will do this" (Isaiah 9:2, 6-7).

See how the Lord kept mixing the story of the coming of the Messiah right into world events.

The greatest moment of my life came when Hezekiah was king of Judah. Now, when you want to talk about great kings, he must be included with the best. He was king when the 10 tribes of Israel north of us made an alliance with Assyria to come down and capture Judah and make us their slaves. As things often happen, that alliance turned against Israel, for Assyria turned against them and made slaves of them. After Assyria had made an end of Israel, we were next. There was no way we could stand against them. They had a huge army, with many horsemen and chariots. They came against us, and we had no chance of beating them back. They laid a siege around Jerusalem, and after many days we began to starve to death.

Hezekiah came often, asking me what to do, and I always told him that the Lord would save us. The people in Jerusalem were lashing out at the king, too. They were saying that Hezekiah did not care what happened to them because, they said, he was eating well and living in comfort, so what did he care! But they changed their attitude when he was walking on the wall of Jerusalem one day, and his cloak fell open. They noticed how gaunt and thin he was. He was also wearing sackcloth on his skin in mourning, and they knew he was suffering more than they.

One night, while I was praying, during that siege, the Lord told me that the next day the siege would be over, and Assyria would be destroyed. I told this to Hezekiah, but he could not believe me. The next day we waited and did not know what had happened. Nothing seemed different, we thought, until four lepers came to the gates of the city and told us their story. They explained to us that they had been starving to death beyond the city wall. They knew it would not be any worse for them if they tried begging from the Assyrians, since they would die anyway without food, so they decided to go to the Assyrian camp to beg for food. They could not believe what they found at the Assyrian camp. A hundred and eighty-five thousand of them were dead in their camp, and the rest of them simply fled from their unknown foe. They had just run away, leaving their tents, their weapons, their food, and all their equipment.

We could hardly believe our ears! We sent out some men to see if it was true, and it was true! The Assyrians were gone. An angel of the Lord had destroyed Assyria in a single night. They never regained their power.

It was the greatest moment of my life. But more significant than that was how the Lord used that occasion to tell me what it would be like when the Christ would reign in the world. He told me there would come forth one day a branch from Jesse—from the son of David—another King. He will be filled with the Spirit of the Lord, He said. He will be filled with wisdom and understanding. His delight will be in the fear of the Lord. He said that when He rules, the wolf will dwell with the lamb; the leopard will lie down with the kid; the lion and the calf and the fatling together; and a little child shall lead them. It will be a day, He said, when a child shall play over the hole of the asp; the suckling child shall put his hand on the adder's den; there will be peace; and the Lord will again save them, as in the day when He saved Judah from Assyria. This One to come would bring peace when their swords will be made into plows, and the spears into pruning hooks, for men will know of war no more. What a description of Christ's kingdom!

That is why I was told by the Lord, "Comfort, comfort My people. Yes, they will go into exile for their sins, but comfort My people, for they are *My* people, and I will yet save them. I will find a way to save them," He said. "I can do it," He said. "Why, I can measure the waters of the earth in the hollow of My hand. I measure the stars with a span of My hand. I have weighed the mountains in My scales, and the nations are like a drop in the bucket to Me." "I can do it," He kept telling me. "I can do it!"

I always wondered how He would do it. How could He save these people? What was the comfort I could give them? They would be so hard to save! How could He save them?

Then He showed me! I could hardly believe it! I could not make anyone in my day believe it. But I saw how He was going to do it. He was going to send His promised Messiah into the world as a servant! The Lord Himself would come to save them! The Son of David who was to be such a great King—a King greater than

David—He was to be a Servant, and a suffering One at that!

I thought, "Who would believe our report?" I was astonished! The heavens were astonished! The Lord bared His arm and was going to act! He would make known His works to all nations. He said to me, "Watchman, lift up your voice and tell them that the Lord will act!" I thought: "How beautiful upon the mountains are the feet of him who brings good tidings, who publishes peace" (Isaiah 52:7).

But who would believe our report? To whom is the arm of the Lord revealed? I saw this One—I saw the Lord Himself grow up before us like a tender plant and like a root out of a dry ground. He had no form or comeliness, that we should look at Him, and no beauty that we should desire Him. I saw that He would be despised and rejected by men, a Man of sorrows and acquainted with grief. As I watched Him in my vision, I knew why He said He would startle the nations when He acts, for as I looked at God Himself here on earth, and what He bore, I hid as it were my face from Him. His appearance was so marred—beyond human semblance—as He would suffer. I began to understand why He said that kings shall stop their mouths at it.

I saw Him oppressed and afflicted, yet He opened not His mouth. Like a sheep before its shearer is dumb, so He opened not His mouth. He was like a lamb led to slaughter. I saw my Lord, stricken, smitten, afflicted! Although there was no deceit in His mouth, and He had done no violence, He was cut off from the land of the living.

I could hardly bear the vision! I wanted to escape the scene, until I suddenly discovered that *it pleased the Lord to bruise Him!* He, the Lord, had put Him to grief! For He had become the offering for sin. Be astounded, O heavens! Be confounded, O nations! Be confused, O rulers! The Lord has found a way to save His people. He shall see the affliction of His Servant and shall see the travail of His soul, and the Lord shall be satisfied. "The Lord has laid on Him the iniquity of us all" (Isaiah 53:6). "Surely, He has borne our griefs, and carried our sorrows. Yet we esteemed Him stricken, smitten by God and afflicted. But He was wounded for our transgressions. He was bruised for our iniquities. Upon Him was the chastisement that made us whole, and with His stripes we are healed" (Isaiah 53:4-5).

Then I saw Him dead! I saw the Lord dead! They made His

grave with the wicked, and with a rich man in His death, although there was no deceit in His mouth and He had done no violence. I saw the Lord, high and lifted up on the cross, and I saw the Lord lowered from the cross and put in a grave. No wonder we hid as it were our faces from Him. Why! So the Lord could find a way to save His people. He was wounded for *our* transgressions. He was bruised for *our* iniquities, and by His stripes *we* are healed. Who would believe it?

That is why I could say, "Ho, everyone who thirsts, come to the waters; and he who has no money, come, buy, and eat. Come, buy wine and milk without money and without price. [It is free—this peace with God.] Why do you spend your money for that which is not bread and your labor for that which does not satisfy? Hearken diligently to me and eat what is good and delight yourselves in fatness. Incline your ear, and come. Hear that your soul may live. [The Lord has found a way to save His people]" (Isaiah 55).

He died for you, and you must believe it. Who has believed our report? To whom is the arm of the Lord revealed? To all who are saved!

8

I, Habakkuk

My name is Habakkuk. It probably does not mean much to you that I lived when Jehoiakim was king of Judah, or that my book is in the Bible between Nahum and Zephaniah. That gives me very little prestige in your minds, does it? But it may come as a surprise to you that my book is being dusted off in your generation, and is being studied very carefully. The reason for that is, that although my book was written for my generation, it could easily have been written for yours. I hope you will understand what I mean as I proceed.

My ministry began the same year as Daniel's, but my ministry lasted only 20 years, whereas Daniel's lasted over 70 years. He survived the Babylonian captivity. I did not. My ministry began the year the Chaldeans from Babylon under Nebuchadnezzar came to Judah the first time in the year 606 B.C., and took some captives to Babylon, among whom were Daniel and Ezekiel. My ministry ended the year Nebuchadnezzar came the second time and made a complete end of my nation by burning and killing, and taking what few survivors were left into captivity.

What makes me such an interesting prophet is the fact that while I served God with all my being, I found it impossible to understand why God did what He did. I just could not understand why God acted the way He did. That is not to say I did not trust Him. It was just that I did not understand Him. Let me tell you about it.

I told you that my ministry began the year the Chaldeans first came from the north and took some of our choicest young men captive. They did that just to show us who was boss and to prove to us who was running the world. They did not do much damage to our land. They just kind of made sport of us because we were so weak.

Now, you would think, wouldn't you, that we in Judah and

Jerusalem would have learned our lesson from that, for God's prophets had told us time and again that this was simply a warning from God that unless we changed, God would make a complete end of our nation. Our leaders were so corrupt, and our people were so greedy and immoral that God was not going to take much more of it. That is why God sent us one warning after another, that if our nation would not straighten up—rulers, religious leaders, and common people—we would no longer be a nation. Finally, the Lord sent us the last warning. It was a partial captivity, but not yet a complete end to our nation.

Well, it didn't help. If anything, the rulers became even more corrupt; the religious leaders, even to a greater extent, told the people what they wanted to hear; and the common people became more and more greedy and immoral.

That, then, became the cause of my first complaint to God. I said: "God, why do you permit that to happen? Why do You continue to let us be ruled by corrupt leaders, and be preached to by false prophets? Why do You let the people get away with being so greedy and immoral? God, why don't You do something about that?" God answered me by saying: "Habakkuk, haven't you noticed, I *am* doing something about it. Get yourself up on a high tower and look north. You will see what I am doing about all this evil and corruption in your land."

I wanted God to do something about the evil in our land, but I was totally unprepared for what He showed me He was going to do. He told me to look north at that nation of Chaldea and be astounded. Believe me, I was! He told me: "I am doing a work in your days that you would not believe if I told you, for lo, I am rousing the Chaldeans, that bitter and vicious nation who will march through the breadth of the earth and seize habitations that are not their own. They are dreadful and terrible who live by no laws but their own and give no justice, only violence to their enemies. They are swifter than leopards and more fierce than wolves. They fly like eagles, and they come only for violence. Terror goes before them. They gather captives like sand, and they laugh at fortresses built against them, for they heap up the earth and take it. They sweep by one enemy after another, and the only god they know is their own might" (Habakkuk 1:5-11 para.).

Do you understand what God was saying to me? He was telling me that He would take care of Judah's corruption by building up a huge, ruthless, terrible kindgom, and that they were going to come down and wipe us out. He told me I should be astonished, and I was! I wished only for our land to be purified. I was not at all prepared to have God tell me that the ancient cursed city where they first tried to build the tower of Babel would now rise up from its ancient ruins and become our masters and destroyers.

That is when I said to God: "How can this be? We are Your chosen people! How can You let such a thing happen to Your chosen people? It isn't fair! It isn't right! Aren't we the people who put our trust in You in the past, and are You going to let that heathen horde overrun us? Lord," I said, "have You ordained *them* as judgment on *us*? Have You established *them* as *our* chastisement? For all our wrongness, we are saints compared to them! We would not think of doing some of the evils they are doing. Have You considered, Lord, the evil of Babylon? Why them, Lord? I want to see my nation straightened out, but I want You to do it, Lord. I don't want an enemy as ruthless as what I have just seen in Babylon to do it."

I must confess, I then tried to embarrass the Lord. I said to Him: "Maybe I have been wrong about You, Lord. I always thought Your eyes were so pure that You would not accept evil. I always thought You would not permit wrong, nor that You would let faithless men succeed. I always thought that You would not stand by when You saw a wicked man swallow up a man who was more righteous than he." Then I said: "I must have been wrong about You, Lord. I must have been misled, for I did not know You delight in torturing innocent people. Have You made us like little fish to be devoured by bigger fish? Are we like worms to be trampled under the feet of the mighty?" I continued: "Those people whom You are calling against us hate not only us—they hate You too! They glory in their idolatry! They boast of the fact that You are not their god and that their gods are better than You are. Listen, Lord, how can You possibly consider letting that happen—that You let *them*, of all people, make an end to us?"

Well, it did happen just as the Lord told me it would. He punished us with a nation much worse than we were. And because it happened the way it did, and because of the reason why God told me it happened, that is why my book is being dusted off today and studied again with great intensity among the theologians in your day. For here, in effect, is what the Lord told me: "Habakkuk, what you say is true. Babylon is ruthless and wicked, more so than any nation before it. They are more evil than your nation ever thought of being. They hate Me, and they enjoy nothing more than ridiculing Me. The fact is, I will take care of the people of Babylon in My own good time, but right now they are serving My purposes. They are My servants. They are the whips that I have chosen to lay across the backs of My own treacherous people. Babylon will go, and its destruction will be terrible, but first Judah goes, for Judah knew what she must do in order to be saved, but she didn't do it. So Judah will go first, and then, in My own good time, Babylon will go. In the meantime, Habakkuk, write this vision. Make it plain on the tablets, so that even when someone is running past it he may read it. Write this: 'Though the vision tarry, wait for it, for the righteous shall live by faith.'"

Now you can see why in days of great sorrow, or great crisis, my book is brought forth and shown to the world again. The problem that confronted me confronts you. You ask, "Why doesn't God act?" You say, "What is going to happen to us?" Yet, you are frightened that God *will* act because of what is happening to this nation of yours, your leaders being what they are, your religion not being what it ought to be, and your morals being so bad. And you notice too how your enemy is getting stronger and stronger. You see it also in your visions.

I wanted to see my nation straightened out, but I did not want it done by an enemy, especially one as ruthless as the one north of us. I didn't want the whole nation to suffer. I only wanted it straightened out, so those who were righteous among us could live with dignity and pride again. So here we stand, you and I together, wondering how God is going to handle it, for handle it He will! It is only a question of how. Does that frighten you?

Listen: If you stand where I stood, you will know that what the Lord told me was the most hopeful and the most uplifting message ever spoken to man. There is not a book in the whole Bible that speaks of such hope as does my book because of the wisdom God gave me to speak. Each prophet had a very distinct message. All of us had messages that overlapped, but we are known for the particular messages we received from the Lord, which we in turn gave to the people. Amos spoke of righteousness. Hosea spoke of

God's love. Jeremiah spoke about personal religion. Isaiah spoke of the Savior to come. I spoke of faith and hope.

After all my complaints to the Lord, this is what He told me to tell you. He said to me: "Habakkuk, you let Me take care of this. I can handle it. You don't have to tell Me what to do or how to do it. You just sit back and watch Me. I am perfectly able to cope with this situation. And that vision you have of better things—though that vision tarry, wait for it. It will come! You just remember that the righteous shall live by faith. You just sit back and wait and have the faith that I will take care of everything. I may not do it right away—though the vision tarry—you just wait for it. I will take care of it, and I will do it right. In the meantime, you live by that faith—the righteous shall live by faith."

The whole New Testament, which is centered in such hope, has as its center the statement that I first made: "The righteous shall live by faith!" When the apostle Paul was trying to put into one verse what the Christian faith was about, he quoted me by saying, "The righteous shall live by faith." When Luther began his Reformation, that was the theme and verse around which the Reformation revolved: "The righteous shall live by faith." They were speaking of the hope that Christ brought, that whoever believes in Him is made righteous in God's sight. I said it before Paul and Luther did.

Ah, yes, in the middle of all that turmoil, when I couldn't figure out why God did what He did, He told me: "Just trust Me. You don't have to know why I do what I do. I will do it right. You'll see." That is why I can say to you that I wrote the most hopeful book ever written, for I said, "Perhaps God does not do things the way we think they should be done, but He does them right."

There is an old tradition that the fathers of the faith insisted was true. It was said that when Daniel was in the lions' den, I came to him and spent the night with him and fed him. Whether I was there in a vision with Daniel or not is unimportant. I just want to say to you that my message was there with him. There was Daniel, facing hungry lions, no doubt wondering why, and wondering too what was to happen to him, but saying in faith what his friends had said when they were going to be thrown into the fiery furnace: "Whether God will save me or not, I do not know, for that is His decision. All I know is, my God can save me if He wishes." He must have heard my message then: "Though the vision tarry, wait for it, for the righteous shall live by faith." I was with him with my message at least.

Ah, I learned so much in those days of crisis, and I have tried to pass it on to you. I was so impatient with the Lord, and He taught me patience. I was so afraid of the future, and He gave me hope. I was questioning God's ways, and He taught Me to trust Him. I hope you have learned that too. God can handle your complaints too. You have had more opportunity to see how God loves you and how He works all things out for your good, than I did. Why, you have even seen such an appalling sight as His Son hanging on a cross dying. If you would have been there, you would have asked the question which I asked: "Why Lord—why did You do that?" He told you through that mighty act of bringing Him back from the dead three days later. "Though the vision tarry, wait for it, for the righteous shall live by faith."

I learned through difficult days and horrible doubts that the Lord always does things right, and I learned to trust Him. That is why I closed my book with words like these:

> I know now, and my body trembles,
> My lips quiver at the sound. . . .
> My steps totter beneath me,
> For I will quietly wait for the day of trouble to come
> upon the enemy who invades us.
> And though the fig tree does not blossom,
> Nor fruit be on the vine,
> And the produce of the olive fail,
> And the fields yield no food,
> And the flock be cut off from the fold,
> And there be no herd in the stalls,
> Yet will I rejoice in the Lord,
> I will still joy in the God of my salvation.
> (Habakkuk 3:16-18 para.)

9
I, Jonah

I am Jonah. Of all the names of prophets in the Old Testament, mine is probably the best-known. I find it amusing that this should be so, since I am remembered mostly because of a fish! Actually, my story is not a story of honor or of heroic deeds, but of stubbornness and meanness. Not that I wasn't a strong prophet. I was strong, as you will see from the results of my preaching—even though it was against my will. But I will speak of that later.

I suppose my name is so well-known because of the controversy that my book has aroused. Many say that my book is a parable, or an allegory, or fiction, or a myth, because they cannot believe that I could have been swallowed by a fish. It arouses my sense of irony that my name should be remembered because of this—a comparatively unimportant event.

That fact is, I was a historical figure. 2 Kings records that I, Jonah, the son of Amittai, was the prophet to Israel during the wicked reign of Jeroboam II. And when Jesus predicted His resurrection, He said: "As Jonah was in the belly of the fish for three days, so must the Son of Man be in the earth three days" (Matthew 12:40 para.). And you know, if the Lord could create a universe, and the earth, and all the creatures of the earth and sea and air, He could certainly create a fish who could swallow and vomit up Jonah. But I did not come to you to rile up the controversy about my book. I have come to you to tell you my story.

I must confess to you that I was not very loving or forgiving. I was very irritable, with a terrible temper. I had a mind of my own, and I even had to be forced by God to do things I did not want to do. But I will tell you one thing—I was a great preacher! It was because I was such a great preacher that God selected me to do a job that I hated above everything else. The job He gave me to do was repulsive! I wasn't very loving in the first place, and then to have to do what God asked me was beyond anything I could stand. God told me to preach in Nineveh! Nineveh! Of all places— Nineveh!

Why, Nineveh was the most wicked city that had ever existed. It was much worse than Sodom and Gomorrah, which God wiped out with fire from heaven in a single day without warning. Now God wanted me to go and warn them in Nineveh that, if they did not repent, the same thing would happen to them. Oh, no! Not I! I wasn't going to go to Nineveh to preach. God could get someone else, but not me!

Why would God want someone to go there to preach anyway? The people there were wicked beyond description. Oh, I know they were great warriors. In the book of Genesis, just after the flood, the man, Nimrod, was mentioned as being the father of the great warriors of the earth. They settled in Nineveh and became those great warriors.

But great warriors have one characteristic. They are mean! They were great warriors because they were so vicious. When they would overrun a nation, they didn't just make slaves of those little nations. They cut off the hands and feet and plucked out the eyes of those they captured. On one occasion they overran a nation, and the warriors remembered that the king's birthday was coming up, so on the king's birthday, he was asked to look out his palace window when he got up in the morning. What he saw pleased him immensely. His warriors had piled up a huge mound of heads—a hill of them—cut off from the bodies of a captured foe after their land was plundered. The king loved it! That is the kind of people they were!

They were mighty and brutal beyond imagination. The prophet Nahum said of them that they were a den of ravenous lions, feeding on the blood of nations. Do you think I would go there to preach? Oh, no! Not Jonah, son of Amittai! So when God told me to preach there, down to the harbor in Joppa I went, and got on a ship to Tarshish, which of course, was in the opposite direction from Nineveh—away, I thought, from the presence of the Lord.

I should have known better. Where can you go away from the presence of the Lord? David had said, "Whither shall I flee from God's Spirit? If I ascend to heaven, He is there. If I make my bed in hell, He is there. If I take the wings of the morning and dwell in the uttermost parts of the sea, even there His hand shall lead me and His right hand hold me" (Psalm 139:7-10) para.) Oh, of all places, to go into the sea to run from God—I should have known better, for God measures the sea in the hollow of His hand (Isaiah 40:12). So there I was, on the sea, in the hollow of God's hand.

Well, you know what happened. God brought forth a great storm on the sea. He was moving His hand, you see, and swirling it around in the hollow of His hand. And there I was, tossed to and fro in the hollow of God's hand.

The sailors on the ship were all pagans, but they sensed something was mysteriously wrong, for they had never experienced such a storm. They all prayed to their gods to help them, but they had no one to help them, for their gods were no gods. Do you know where the captain found me during that storm? I was down in the hold, sleeping. When he found me, he shook me, and said to me, "What are you doing down here sleeping, when you ought to be praying to your God to save us?"

The pagans have to say that to us once in a while, don't they? They are working and struggling so hard in the world, but they don't have any answers to all the problems we face. Only we who worship the true God have the answers, and that answer is found in praying to the true God, who can do anything He wants. You must understand why I did not want to talk to God right then. I was running from Him. The farther I got from Him, the safer I felt I would be.

So they drew lots to find out whose fault all this trouble was, and naturally, it fell on me. They said, "Who are you, anyway? What is your occupation? Where are you from? What have you done?" I told them, "I am a Hebrew, a prophet, and I am fleeing from the presence of the Lord." They asked me what they should do, for the sea was growing more and more tempestuous. I said, "Throw me overboard and the sea will quiet down."

You can see, I was no coward. Some of you may think that is why I did not want to go to Nineveh, because I was a coward. Oh, no! I was no coward. That was not why I did not want to go to Nineveh.

The sailors finally had to throw me overboard, and when they did, the sea quieted. You have to do that once in a while. There are some people who cause so much trouble, whether in the world, or in the church, or in the family, that the ship sometimes cannot survive the troubles caused by that individual. He must be thrown overboard for the sake of the rest, and if God wants to save him, He will. You have to come to the point where you commit them to God and let God take care of it.

Down into the sea I went, and the sea calmed. I described in my book how I felt, going down there into the bottom of the sea where the roots of the mountains are, and the weeds wrapped about my head, and the sea closed in over me.

Do you know what I thought of going down there? I thought of the temple of God in Jerusalem that Solomon had built, and I wondered if I would ever see that place again where God made His presence known. Do you think it strange that my thoughts turned to that temple? I tell you, that temple was everything to me, and I couldn't bear the thought of not seeing it again. Some of you may feel that way about your church too.

It was not the beauty of the temple I missed so much as it was the fact that it was where I could best feel the presence of God. That was what I missed. In fact, what I feared at that moment was that I would never again see the presence of God. How could I have tried to run away from that? He was the most precious thing of my life. How could I have tried to run from Him? I repented down there for my foolishness.

You know what happened then. The Lord sent a fish that swallowed me, and three days later it vomited me up on the shore. The voice of God came to me again on the shore: "Jonah, son of Amittai, go to Nineveh and preach to that wicked city." This time I did it. I still did not want to, you understand, but what could I do after all the trouble God took to straighten me out? You would have gone too, wouldn't you?

I will never forget walking into that great city. I had never seen anything like it except in visions. It was 30 miles long and 10 miles wide, with 5 walls surrounding it, and 3 canals, all built with the labor of captives whose hands, feet, and heads had not yet been cut off. There was limitless wealth everywhere, poured in from the ends of the earth. The inner city, where the palaces, princes, kings, and armies were, was three miles long and one and a half miles wide, with a wall 100 feet high surrounding it. That wall was wide enough for four chariots to race side by side at the same time. It was an astounding sight there by the Tigris River.

There I walked on those streets, back and forth, saying: "Yet 40 days, and Nineveh shall be overthrown. Yet 40 days, and Nineveh will be overthrown." When I was finished I went outside the city and sat on a hill, where I waited for the rest of those 40 days, just waiting for the fire to come down from heaven and destroy that brutal, monstrous city. I can't tell you how angry I was at what happened! I told you that I was a great preacher. I wasn't very loving, nor was I forgiving, but I was a great preacher! Those people in that wicked city repented because of my preaching! News reached the king about what I had said, and he called for a national period of fasting, and he covered himself with sackcloth and sat on ashes, and he ordered the people of the city to do the same thing.

That's when I blew my stack! I told the Lord: "I knew it! I knew it all the time! Isn't this what I told You when I was still in my own country? That is why I tried to get away from You in Tarshish. I told You so! I told You that if I went to this people to preach—and You know what kind of preacher I am—and I know what kind of a God You are—I told You that they would repent and You would forgive them. I knew You were loving and forgiving, and You would not destroy them if I came here to preach! I knew it all the time!! I would have been better off, and the world would have been better off if I would have drowned in the sea! I wish I were dead!" The Lord simply said to me, "Jonah, do you do well to be angry?" I said, "Yes, angry enough to die!"

I still couldn't believe it. So I sat there, east of the city, for a while, my head getting sunburned, and the Lord had some mercy on me. He had a plant grow over my head in one day which spread its shade over me, and my bald head was more comfortable there in the shade, and I felt a little better. I was happy to have the plant. But that very night, God had a little worm bore into the base of the plant—and the plant died! Then, besides that, He sent a hot, sultry wind and hot sun on my head until I was ready to faint.

By now, I wasn't in a very good mood, so I said: "What's with it here, God? Why did You do that? All this trouble about going to Nineveh in the first place. Then not destroying that wicked city. And now—this is the last straw—You take my plant away from me! Why don't You just let me die and get it over with!"

God said to me again, "Jonah, do you do well to be angry about that little plant?" "Yes," I said, "angry enough to die. After all I have gone through, now You take away my plant!"

Then God said to me: "Jonah, that was not your plant. It was

My plant. You did not plant it, you did not make it grow, you did not make it die. It was My plant to do with as I please. That is the way it is with Nineveh. Those are My people. You did not create them. I did. You did not labor over them. I did. And Jonah—many there are only children. Have I not the right to pity them if I wish?"

That is the way my book ends. I wasn't a very good prophet, was I? But I was a good preacher, and the Lord knew whom to send to the people of that wicked city so He could have mercy on them. Aren't you glad that the Lord isn't like we are? Where would any of us be if the Lord treated us like I wanted to treat Nineveh. As I look back at it now, I realize that it took as much grace to save me as it did to save Nineveh. I was a terrible prophet. I had a terrible temper. I was unloving. I had no forgiveness in my heart. I tried to run from God. I attacked God for what He did. Yet, God had mercy on me and saved me. Your Jesus proves God's love for you, and because of Jesus, even a Nineveh can be saved and forgiven. Yes, even a Jonah can be saved and forgiven.

Are you interested in what happened to me? One of my successors as prophet was a man named Nahum, who lived 150 years after me. He gave much the same message to Nineveh as I did, for the people there were even more wicked in his day than they were in mine. But this time they did not repent. The Lord therefore sent Babylon against them to besiege that mighty city and its great warriors.

While Babylon was laying siege to Nineveh, one night a great storm came, and the Tigris river rose to such a height that it swept away the walls of the city. Even with their great warriors, they could not save their city because they had no way to protect themselves, so Babylon crushed that city so badly that it disappeared from the face of the earth. It was worse for them than it was for Sodom and Gomorrah. In fact, it was so completely wiped out that even the ruins of that city were not found for 2,500 years. Until the year 1850 A.D., all evidence of that city was lost. In that year an archeologist from England discovered the ruins of the city. That is why, for so many years, many scholars thought my story to be a myth. They thought that Nineveh did not exist in my day.

But let me conclude. In the ruins of the city there is a mound that has been unearthed which has the inscription: "Jonah's Mound." It is believed to be my burial place. Isn't it strange that I should have become so famous in Nineveh that they brought my body there to be buried, since it was the place of my greatest triumph? Our God certainly works in strange ways to demonstrate His mercy.

10
I, Micah

I am Micah. I have gone down in history as a minor prophet, but in the days when we were preaching, none of us thought of ourselves as major or minor prophets. We just did and spoke the things we were called to do and speak. Each of us was given a message from God to deliver, and we just did it. As a matter of fact, none of us ever thought we would go down in history as being great. We just lived in our little corner of the world and tried to do our job as best we could. It was as simple as that.

It was just that we lived during a time when the world was in a period of great crisis, and we were caught up in that crisis. I lived my life as a God-fearing man in my day, you live your lives as God-fearing people in yours. Who knows what history will record about you? More important than that, who knows what heaven will say about you when your life's course is run? It is history, by the way, about which I have come back to talk to you.

I hope you know the history of my people. After David and Solomon were dead, our nation of Israel was divided into the northern and southern kingdoms. The Northern Kingdom fell in the year 721 B.C. to the Assyrians, never to be a nation or kingdom again. The Southern Kingdom was able to survive for another 140 years.

The Northern Kingdom was unbelievably wicked. That is why God made an end to it. He simply was not going to take that from people whom He had so blessed. I lived in the Northern Kingdom, and I saw it all happen. When that kingdom fell, I came down to the Southern Kingdom to preach. I was the only prophet to preach in both kingdoms. I was a contemporary of Amos and Hosea in the North, and of Isaiah in the South. I was in pretty good company, wouldn't you say?

Now, in a way, I could understand how the Northern Kingdom

could have fallen. God had blessed its people all those years because they were His chosen people. Even when they sinned terribly and became terribly wicked, they still held to the false notion that God would bless them anyway, no matter how immoral and greedy they became. "How could God give up His own children?" they used to say. Even though Amos and Hosea had warned them so sternly, I can perhaps understand why they would not listen, for they had no history that would have told them that God will not let a nation like that survive.

Oh, they had some history during the time of Joshua and the Judges to let them know that God would not permit a nation to live that way, but God had never made a complete end to them before. Now He had! He had done it! History recorded it for everyone to see and interpret. A nation that rejects God and His ordinances cannot survive.

That is why I was so stunned when I came down to the Southern Kingdom of Judah and found they had not learned the lesson of history. Anyone who wants to interpret history can readily see that when immorality, greed, dishonest rulers, and dishonest judges take over a nation, it will not survive. If there is a God in heaven, He will let no such nation continue to exist. History always tells us that in whatever period you study it. But those people down there in the Southern Kingdom saw what had happened up north, and they continued to live the same way.

For that reason, I did an astounding thing when I went to Jerusalem to preach. I walked among them naked, and I preached to them naked! I did that, of course, to attract attention—and you can imagine that I did! We had to do things in those days that your prophets in your day do not have to do. We did anything and everything in those days to make the people listen, because we were living in days of terrible crisis. My purpose, of course, was not just to attract attention. I was trying to remind the people in Jerusalem what had happened to us up north. We were stripped naked by an enemy because we did not remain faithful to God.

I remember hearing the prophet Hosea preach. He was the one, you remember, whom the Lord ordered to marry a harlot because the Lord wanted him to tell the people what it was like having a wife who was not faithful to him, who ran after every other man she could, and who gave her body to anyone who wanted her. God wanted Hosea to tell them what it felt like to love someone who did not return that love, but went whoring after every corruption she could find. God wanted Hosea to experience that, so he could tell the people how God felt. God told the people through Hosea that if they didn't stop whoring after those other gods, He would strip them naked so everyone could see their shame. That is just what God had to do!

Well, here I came, after God had stripped us naked for being unfaithful to Him all those years—here I came before those people in the South, naked. I tried to impress upon them that they could not ignore history. I tried to tell them that what happened in history will happen again to an unfaithful nation. We had been caught in our harlotry! We were guilty! The Lord Himself had testified against us! We had been caught red-handed! Now God sent me to tell them in the South that He had caught them also in harlotry. You cannot ignore history, I said.

I also came before them naked because I was representing a group of people who were being taken advantage of by the rich and by the rulers and judges in Jerusalem. Nearly all of the leadership in the South was in Jerusalem. It was a small kingdom now, and the leadership was centralized in the capital city. Isaiah was in Jerusalem trying to straighten out things with the leadership of the nation, but my concern was with the common people in the countryside. Although Isaiah made some references to the poor, his concern was more with the powerful among us. You see, Isaiah was from the city and of royal lineage. I was from the country, from a small town about 20 miles southwest of Jerusalem called Moresheth. I saw what was happening to the common people.

The rich and the powerful from Jerusalem were buying up and taking the land away from the weak and poor. When the poor would take the rich to court, the judges were paid off by the rich, so the poor lost their land and they had nothing to live by. The rich were stripping the poor naked, and I represented the poor. The Lord called me to be the judge, and He said He would witness against them, because, He said: "My glory is tied up with the poor."

Do you understand what He meant? This is what the Lord told me: "These poor, meek people trust Me. I gave that land to their fathers, and to their fathers before them, and I protected their land with My laws so that no one would be able to take that land from them. That land has belonged to their families since the day I gave them this land when they came out of bondage in Egypt. The land is their birthright, and it is where their families have buried their forefathers. These people trust Me to keep it for them. How dare the rich and the powerful take it from them!"

"These are simple people," He said, "who trust Me. I promised them security and peace, and I promised them that they would be able to keep this land as long as they wished. And now, you—you rich and powerful—you would take it from them? Do you think I will stand for that?"

The Lord was furious! He said, "I gave them that land! You have no right to it! The land is for Me to give and take, and those people trust Me to keep them safe, and now you take that trust from them? You are destroying My glory when you cause them to lose their land, because I promised it to them. It is My glory you are messing with here. Shall I forgive you for that? No! You rich and powerful—you will eat, but you will never be satisfied. You will put away, but you will never save anything. And what you save will be taken away from you with the sword. I will not take that from you," says the Lord. "Those people trust Me, and you are taking away their trust in Me."

As I stood there telling them this, I said: "With what shall I come before the Lord? Shall I come before Him with burnt offerings? Shall I give my firstborn for my transgression? No, He has showed you, O man, what is good; and what does the Lord require of you but to do justice, and to love kindness, and to walk humbly with your God?" (Micah 6:6-8).

It was then that the Lord told me something that the world had been waiting to know for a long, long time. He told me where His Son was to be born—this One who was to save His people from sin—this Ancient of Days, who was to cause the glory of the Lord to show forth in Zion. I was told where He would be born! He who would bring forth a day when men would know peace, when they would beat their swords into plowshares, and their spears into pruning hooks, and men would know of war no more—I was told where He was to be born!

We had always thought He would be born in Jerusalem. After all, it was the capital city. It was the place where David had established his rule. It was David's "City of Peace." Even the Wise Men, when they came from the East, thought He would be born in Jerusalem. But not so!

As the Lord spoke to me about Jerusalem and the wickedness

of that city when its people took advantage of the poor and stole their land, the Lord told me that His Son would not make His entrance there. Jerusalem, He said, would take a rod and strike Him upon the cheek, but He would not be born there. He would be born in Bethlehem of Judea, a simple little village, with simple people, who had been taken advantage of by the rich and powerful in Jerusalem.

It was as if God made that decision in my day when He saw how the rich and proud took advantage of the poor who trusted Him. It was not to be that such glory would go to Jerusalem. It was to be that such glory would go to the little town of Bethlehem. Jerusalem had had all the advantages. The priests were there—the kings—the prophets. But the Lord turned aside from all that glory and gave the glory to the humble and meek. No wonder He said: "Blessed are the meek, for they shall inherit the earth." No wonder, too, His mother said: "My soul magnifies the Lord, and my spirit rejoices in God my Savior, for He has regarded the low estate of His handmaiden." You see, God's glory is tied up with the poor, the simple, the humble who trust Him, and He makes His glory known through them.

Actually, it was fitting that the Ancient of Days be born in Bethlehem. It was the birthplace of David. It was also where our patriarch Jacob buried his beloved wife Rachel, as she died giving birth to Benjamin. That is why, when Jeremiah predicted that Herod would try to kill Jesus by killing all the male children in Bethlehem under two years of age, he said: "Rachel will weep for her children, but no one can comfort her, for they are not" (31:15). He was to be born in Bethlehem.

You will notice, when you read my book, how difficult it is to read, for I keep going back and forth between God's judgment and His mercy. In the same breath I spoke of His judgment, and then of His mercy, and then back to His judgment again. Can you understand why I did that? God is severe on those who take advantage of His people, but He is so merciful with His own! I could never speak of God's judgment without, in the same breath, speaking of His love and mercy. I could never divide them, for God always shows mercy, even in His days of judgment.

Your own preachers who know the Christ can never speak of the sins of the people without speaking of God's love for you in His Son. That is why I was always back and forth from judgment to mercy. You can sort it out if you like, but even in the days of my greatest frustration, I could never stop telling them about the forgiveness and love of God, even for the worst of God's people. That is why I finished my prophecy with this prayer: "Who is a God like You, pardoning iniquity and passing over transgression? You will cast all our sins into the depths of the sea. You will show faithfulness to Jacob and steadfast love to Abraham, as You have sworn to our fathers from days of old."

11
I, Zechariah

I am Zechariah. If you know anything at all about the prophets of old, you will know that I was unique among them. I lived in days of great hope and expectation. I was the one who told God's people, "Everything is O.K." I was the one whose message was: "God is only going to bless you. You need not fear anything, for God is going to bless you." Do you know why I was able to say that and still be true to God as a prophet?

Other prophets in other days were rebuked mightily for saying the same thing. As a matter of fact, that was a major cause of God's greatest wrath when prophets in other days used to say: "Don't worry, God will always bless you." That made God very angry. But, you see, it was a new day when I lived. It was a day of great hope, and we saw nothing ahead of us but God's blessings. It was the message God called me to deliver. It was a brand new day.

Solomon once said: "There is a time for everything under the sun. There is a time to be born, and a time to die; . . . a time to kill, and a time to heal; a time to break down, and a time to build up; a time to weep, and a time to laugh; a time to mourn, and a time to dance; . . . a time for war, and a time for peace" (Ecclesiastes 3:1-8). Well, we had had our times to kill and break down and weep and mourn. We had had our time of war. But now it was a time for peace and a time to heal and to laugh and dance. I was the prophet privileged to be born and to preach in such days.

Most of the other prophets lived in days of great peril and evil in our land. They had to preach in perilous times concerning their evil, and they had to warn the people of God that if they didn't turn around, God would bring them into bondage. It was the false prophets who said in those days that everything was alright, but the true prophets announced doom.

But that was all over now. It was a new day, and the Lord said,

"I have chastised My people enough. It is time to let them go back home." So Darius, king of Persia, who had conquered Babylon, in the year 563 B.C. wrote out a decree that we were allowed to be free and go home—free from bondage. So after 70 years of bondage, 50,000 of us went back to Jerusalem.

It was a great day to be alive. Oh, we had our difficulties, but we knew, because God's anger with us had subsided, and because He had blessed us by permitting our return, that we would be blessed.

It was such a pleasant thing, being a prophet in my day. Other prophets of God who spoke God's truth in other days were persecuted and beaten and abused and killed, all because they had to tell the people what they did not want to hear. I was loved because I could tell the people what they wanted to hear—that God loved them and had forgiven them and would bless them. It was nice being able to preach such a message. And along with that, the people were so happy. They didn't have any rulers to tax them. They had no armies to supply, because our enemies were weak. All we needed and wanted was God, and we knew we had Him.

In order for me to tell you why my ministry was so pleasant, I must tell you about Haggai, who was also a prophet in my day. Haggai was a very old man when we came back from bondage. In fact, it is said of him that he was taken into bondage 70 years earlier as a young boy, and lived there in bondage all those existing years waiting and praying that he could be one of those returning from exile. God permitted that old man to come back with us. His ministry lasted only four months back in Jerusalem, and my ministry, as a young man, overlapped his by two months. We worked together only two months, but I reaped the harvest of his rich ministry.

Let me explain. When we came back from exile, the first thing we started to do was to rebuild the temple. We knew that if we were to be the kind of people we were supposed to be, we would have to have a place to worship. So we immediately built the foundation of the temple in Jerusalem. When our enemies around Jerusalem discovered what we were doing, they began to make threats to us. They told us that if we rebuilt the temple they were going to come over with their armies and destroy us. They knew that worship in the temple would bring us together and make us strong. They had very good reason for believing that, and so they tried to stop us.

Well, we were a weak people, with little courage after all those years in exile, and we knew we had no way to defend ourselves, so we gave up building the temple. That foundation stood there for 15 years without any work done on it. The vines and the dirt began covering the foundation, and everyone seemed to forget about it. Our enemies left us alone, and everything seemed to be alright.

Those of us who came back from captivity went about the business of building our own homes and taking care of our farms, but we always knew something was wrong. We were not progressing as we thought we should. Then one day, the old man Haggai spoke to us, and his four months of ministry began. He said: "The Lord has spoken to me and said to me that the people are saying that it is not yet time to rebuild the temple. 'Is it time,' He said, 'to build your own homes and be comfortable while the house of God lies in ruins? Consider this,' He said, 'how you have fared. You sow much, but you harvest little; you eat, but you never have enough; you drink, but you never have your fill; you clothe yourselves, but you are never warm; you earn wages, but you put it into a bag with holes. Consider how you have fared,' the Lord said, 'for nothing is right with you because My house is in ruins. Go build My house,' says the Lord."

It was remarkable for me to notice that the very day when Haggai spoke, the people went into the hills and forests and began bringing the supplies to Jerusalem to build the temple, and they never left off until it was finished.

It was not much of a temple. Solomon's was much more magnificent. The people actually wept when it was finished, because they remembered Solomon's temple, and this was so small compared to it. Haggai himself had seen Solomon's temple before it was destroyed, and although there was joy for him when the new one was begun again, he felt great anguish that it could not compare to the one he remembered in his youth.

That is what I inherited. You must know what it is like when people get together on a great project. They are of one mind and one spirit. They enjoy working together. They are happy to make the sacrifice. There is nothing like it among the people of God! Besides that, we had the assurance that God was blessing us, and would continue to bless us because of our work on His sanctuary. Ah, if you have ever experienced that, you know there is never a time like it! You talk about it to your children and your children's children after you. What a great day it was, when we dedicated the temple of the Lord! Can you imagine what it was like for me to be permitted to stand before God's people on the day of dedication and say to them: "From this day forward, the Lord will bless you because of the temple you have built for Him at great sacrifice?"

Not every generation of men is permitted to experience such ecstasy. It is as the Lord told me: "Does a prophet live forever?" No. Each generation must have its own prophets. Each generation must begin again to build its own temples, whatever they may be, so that they too can feel the assurance of God's blessings and love. You must do that in your own generation—build your own temples— for if you don't, the Lord withholds many of His blessings.

We were shown that very vividly when the generation of Moses' day didn't have the faith to go over into the promised land to take it. The blessings were reserved for the next generation, who said: "Sure, we can take that land! The Lord said He would be with us, so we can take it!" The blessings came to them because they had the faith to take it. A prophet does not live on earth forever. Each generation must have its own prophets who are listened to and followed, and if they are not followed—if the people do not build their own temples, they will not receive the blessings they could have.

My day was a great day to be alive! We were filled with hope! We were filled with hope because of what you already know. We knew the Lord would send His Messiah, and when the Messiah would come He would set the world right, and the world would never lose its hope. We were all thinking of that in our day. That is why in those days of great hope, I had one vision after another of the greatness of the Kingdom, which our Messiah would establish. In days of hope our minds always turned to the Messiah.

I had visions of a red horse that ranged through the earth and came back to me with the message that the world was at peace. I saw a young man with a measuring line trying to measure Jerusalem, and an angel stopped him, saying to him: "You can't measure Jerusalem! It will become so great that no one can measure it, for not only the Jews will flow into it but all nations will come from all parts of the world to worship there and dwell there." I also had a vision of that little temple of ours too. The Lord told me that the temple He would build in other days would be people— people would be His temple.

I saw another vision of my high priest, Joshua, standing before God in tattered, filthy clothing, with Satan beside him, accusing him of being evil and claiming Joshua as his own. Now, you must understand that Joshua was our high priest—he represented us. We were the ones standing beside Satan being accused, and Satan *did* have a right to us. We had been very evil. What would you expect? We deserved to be claimed by Satan, and he felt he had a perfect right to us.

It was with great satisfaction, therefore, that I heard the Lord say to Satan: "The Lord rebukes you, Satan, for I have chosen Jerusalem. Do you not know, Satan, that this is a brand from the burning? I have plucked him out of the fire. In a single day," the Lord said, "I will take his iniquity from him." Then the Lord turned to Joshua in my vision and said: "Therefore I have taken away your iniquity, Joshua, and I put new clothing on you. And hear now, O Joshua," the Lord said, "you and your friends; I will set you on a stone, and I will bring My servant to you to save you in a single day."

You saw that day, didn't you, when God sent His Messiah to you to cleanse you from all sin in a single day on a cross. I saw that in a vision. I can't tell you what it meant to us. You saw it happen! I wonder what it means to you?

Permit me just one more word. When the temple was finished, a group of people came to the temple asking us if they should continue to fast on the days that had been appointed for fasting. They asked that in good faith, for they truly wanted to know if they should continue to fast to please the Lord. I asked the Lord about that, and this is what He told me to tell them: "When you used to fast, why did you do it? You really did it for yourselves to make you feel better. You fasted on certain days, because you wanted Me to forgive you. You wanted Me to forgive you, because you felt that gave you the right to sin some more, and as long as you fasted, you continued in your sin. You did it for yourselves, you didn't do it for Me," the Lord said.

"No, I don't want your fasting," He said. "I want you to live righteously so that your old men and your old women can sit in the streets in safety and in comfort, and your young children can play in your streets without fear. If you would be righteous, then all of you will be happy. That is what I want. I want My people to live in peace and contentment. They will be able to live that way if you are righteous and if you won't take advantage of one another." Then the Lord spoke of the temple: "When you come to the temple, I don't want you to come here to fast. I want you to come in joy and celebration. I don't want you coming to My temple fasting in order that I will forgive your sins. Don't you understand? I have already forgiven your sins! Why do you think you have to fast to try to convince Me to forgive you? I have already forgiven you! It is a new day! I have done what I said I would do! I have forgiven your sins in a single day! Don't come now to ask for forgiveness! I have given you that. Come now in celebration!"

That is what the Lord told me to tell them in that new day of hope. It was good news, and it was what the people wanted to hear. But do you know, I could never convince them of that. It was what they wanted to hear, but they could never quite believe it. They kept right on fasting more and more, thinking that if they fasted, the Lord would bless them more.

I know in your day the prophets have the same problem. Your prophets keep telling you that you are forgiven. Your Christ has paid for your sins and you are totally forgiven. All the Lord asks is that you believe it and trust Him, and celebrate it, and you like to hear your prophets telling you that, don't you?

But isn't it terrible to have Satan keep standing beside you accusing you, trying to convince you that you have to do more than just believe it. Satan makes you believe that you have to do more than just celebrate it. That is what takes your hope and joy from you. You love to hear your prophets tell you the good news of how God has saved you and forgiven you, but you just have so much trouble believing it!

I wonder why you let Satan do that to you? God has told you in such an emphatic way that you are forgiven in Christ. How can you let Satan curse you with such feelings of guilt, when God has blessed you with such hope? That new day of hope which I said was coming? That new day is yours! Don't let anyone take it from you!

12
I, Malachi

I am the last prophet. I am Malachi. For 400 years after I died, God did not speak to any prophet until John the Baptist came to prepare the world for the Christ. That made me a prophet of great importance, for my message had to serve God's people for a long time. Had they heeded the Word that the Lord gave me, it would have served them for those 400 years. There wasn't anything else to be said until our Messiah appeared. As I have come back to your generation, I find it ironic that if I were a prophet in your day, I would have to change very little of my message, for I see in your generation what I saw in mine.

But before I speak my message again, let me give you some of the background of my ministry. In the year 536 B.C., Darius, king of Persia permitted my Jewish ancestors to come back to Jerusalem out of bondage. About 50,000 of them came back with the prophets Haggai and Zechariah. Twenty years after the return, they finished building their temple, so they had a place to worship. That was a great day of hope!

But you know how it is. The generation that built the temple found great satisfaction in the sacrifices they made to build it. They worshiped in that temple every opportunity they had. But that generation of workers died, and the next generation did not have to make the kind of sacrifices for their privilege to worship that the previous generation had to make, so they took their worship for granted. The third generation after the dedication of the temple didn't even bother to worship, for they paid no price at all for that privilege. When their grandparents would tell them about the satisfaction they had when they built the temple and worshiped in it, the people of this third generation removed just kind of smiled and went their way.

It was to the third and fourth generations removed from the

dedication of the temple that my message was directed, because I was the prophet who preached about 100 years after the temple was finished.

In the time between the dedication of the temple and when I was a prophet, some important events concerning my people were taking place in Persia. Only a small fraction of my ancestors came back from Persia to resettle Jerusalem in 536 B.C. Over a million Jews did not come back. They stayed in the lands where they had been help captive.

Well, it so happened that the son of Darius, Ahasuerus, who became king of Persia and thus of the world, married a very beautiful woman named Esther. She was a Jewess. You can see how important we Jews became in that Persian Empire, for not only was the Queen a Jewess, also the Prime Minister was a Jew named Mordecai.

I am certain you know the story of Esther, how one of the administrators of King Ahasuerus so hated the Jews that, by deceit and craft, he had the king sign an edict that would have had all the Jews in the whole empire killed. Esther saved us because of the king's love for her. Then her son became the next king of the empire, and because of her influence, when Nehemiah, the cupbearer of the king, asked to have an army go back with him to Jerusalem to protect Jerusalem from our enemies, the king gladly obliged. When Nehemiah came to Jerusalem, we had a leader.

Ezra, our high priest, also came back just before Nehemiah. It was the three of us who tried to put our nation back together again. I was a prophet; Ezra was a priest; Nehemiah was a ruler. All three of us were totally dedicated to the Lord.

It sometimes seemed to the three of us that we were the only ones in the land who were so dedicated. There were times when no one else seemed to care. I do not mean that the people were worshiping idols. The Jews never again worshiped idols after the exile. Never again did the Jews ever worship a foreign god. It was just that they became so careless in their religion! Their religion did not cost them anything, so they took it all for granted! What their parents and grandparents sacrificed so much for, this generation took for granted. They just became too careless in religious matters. When you begin to take your religion for granted, it will happen every time—you become careless.

If you will read the books of Ezra and Nehemiah and my book, you will know how disturbed we were with this, and what we did about it. Nehemiah went to work getting the people to rebuild the walls of Jerusalem. Those walls had lain in ruins for 150 years. There had not been enough pride and courage among us to rebuild them. So Nehemiah put the people to work. That was important, for they had to be reminded what it was like to sacrifice again for their city and for their faith and for their heritage.

But more important than that was what concerned Ezra and me. Three major problems confronted us with the people. If we were again to be a great nation, and if we were to accomplish what the Lord told me to tell them: "Return to Me and I will return to you, says the Lord"—if that was to happen, then we were going to have to do something about those three problems.

First of all was the matter of the priests. The priests were not being faithful! I do not mean that they were like the priests before the exile, who set up idols everywhere, even in the temple of God. Our priests never did that again. It was just that the priests in my day were so careless! They handled sacred things as if they were nothing! They had been called to their high office and were given all the benefits of it, but they didn't even half try to lead the people in the right direction. They were just so careless! They were not teaching God's Word, because they didn't take the trouble to know it for themselves. They were called to be God's mouth, but they didn't know what God's Word said, so how could they teach it?

Do you know what those priests said? They said: "It is too much trouble." They said, "It is tiresome—what weariness this is!" That is how they felt about the priesthood! It was too much trouble for them to do it well! What a terrible attitude! Of course, if they felt that way about the Word, which they were to teach, they would feel that way about everything, including the sacrifices that people brought.

Those people brought in the worst-looking sacrifices you could imagine. If they had a blind sheep, that is what they offered to the Lord as their offering. If an ox or a cow would break a leg, they brought that in to the Lord as their offering. They even brought in dead cattle and dead sheep that had died in their pastures or barns, and they offered them to the Lord. They thought they were giving the Lord an acceptable offering when they brought in those miserable creatures. Do you know why the people thought they could offer those kind of sacrifices to the Lord? Because the priests accepted them! It was too much trouble not to accept those offerings, they said. It was too tiresome to tell the people that they would have to do better than that.

You know how people are. They will get by with the least they can get by with. They must have someone tell them what is acceptable and what is not, or they will do the least possible things they can do.

The priests were God's mouth. It was their responsibility to tell the people that those offerings were not acceptable. The priests were to be God's spokesmen. But they said, "It is too much trouble. The people won't like us if we tell them that." That is why I told them, "Don't you know that is the reason people have such contempt for you, because you don't tell them? That is why people don't come to you, because they know they will not get it straight from you! Even the seed you sow will rot before it takes root, because you are so careless with the sowing. If you would do your job, without being so careless and lazy, the people would not only do better, but you would have the respect which is due your office."

That is why Ezra, when he came from Persia, was so appalled. One of his forefathers was once our high priest, Hilkiah, who worked with Isaiah and king Hezekiah when there was a great reformation in Judah. If you ever want to hear about the combination of a prophet, priest, and king—those three were something! Ezra was a worthy successor to Hilkiah. He immediately called the priests together and let them have it! He spoke more harshly to them than I did, for he was one of them. He spent months teaching them the Word and the duties of their office. Then those priests called the people together every day for seven straight days, and they studied the Word with the people of the land, and together they learned again the will of the Lord. In this way the priests regained their honor among the people, and the people learned the Word.

The second problem that Ezra and I faced was the deterioration of the marriage vows. Since they were so careless about their religion, they were careless about other important things also. Of course, the first place where lack of the knowledge of God's will shows up is in family life. If you are careless about God, how can you expect to be faithful to your family? You see, it is a matter of being faithful. It is a pattern you learn to live by. If you are not faithful to God, you can expect faithfulness nowhere.

In our day, women had no rights. They were simply considered to be property. They were considered to be possessions of their men. That is why it was so devastating to the women in my day when many of the men decided that if they got tired of their wives, they would just get another one. Or if another woman looked good to them, they would discard the wife of their youth and marry another. Those husbands often brought other women into their own homes and made their wives share their affections with another. If the wife objected, they simply divorced them. Many of them married foreign women who brought their gods with them. Now, if the Lord would not take that kind of treatment for Himself from the people, He certainly would not permit the men to treat their wives that way either.

The Lord told me to tell them two things about that: He said, "I have heard the weeping and the wailing of the wives who have been put away. I will not bless you until the sound of that weeping and wailing ceases." If the Lord could hear Abel's blood crying out from the ground after Cain had killed him, He could also hear the weeping and wailing of wives who had been put away at the whim of their husbands!

The Lord told me a second thing too: "The children—what is to happen to the children of these marriages? How can a child be taught faithfulness if the parents are unfaithful? What will come of the seed of the marriage?" He said. "I want faithful children," God said, "and how can they learn faithfulness, growing up in that sort of atmosphere?" You see, not only the wives suffered. The children suffered as well because of the unfaithfulness of the husbands and fathers.

Well, after Ezra got the priests straightened out, and those priests taught the people the Word in its truth, you can imagine how quickly it followed that this matter of unfaithfulness to a man's wife ceased. Ezra called the leaders of the people together and told them that all the men in Jerusalem who married second wives would have to give them up and go back to the wife of their youth. Likewise, all who married foreign wives would have to give them up. And they did! Almost to a man, they did it! You see, if the Word of God is taught and learned in its purity, the other problems straighten themselves out easily. If one becomes faithful to God through the knowledge of His Word, he will become faithful in other matters too. Only the Word of God has the power to change lives. When the Word of God is neglected or used carelessly, everything else falls apart. But if it is known and lived by, everything comes together. The matter of the husbands being unfaithful was easily solved by the knowledge of the Word.

But the third matter was quite different. It was not so easily solved, even when the Word had been taught. Perhaps you in your day can imagine what it was—it was the matter of the giving of the people. We were instructed by the law of Moses that we were to give 10 percent of our earnings to the Lord. It was called the tithe. When I spoke to the people about that, I got resistance. Even after they knew the law of Moses, which stated that very plainly, I still got resistance.

They kept telling me, "Why should we tithe? We are no better off if we give the tithe than if we don't. In fact, we can't afford to give that much back to the Lord." Then they brought this up to me: "Those heathen neighbors of ours," they said, "they don't tithe, and they are getting along alright. Why should we tithe? We can't afford to tithe."

The Lord told me to tell them, "Will a man rob God?" The people said: "We cannot rob God." God said: "Oh, yes, if you do not bring me your tithes, you rob Me of what belongs to Me."

You know, our people were too religious to rob their neighbors. In my day, no one would think of robbing his neighbors. It was against God's law. But they did not mind robbing God! Can you imagine that? That is why the Lord told me to tell them: "You say it is of no advantage to you to tithe. I say to you, 'Test Me! Bring your tithes into My storehouse and see if I will not pour you out a blessing, that you will not be able to contain it all. Test Me! See if it is not true!'" As you know, we convinced them to tithe, and it became one of the great tenets of our religion.

I earlier mentioned to you that I was the last of the prophets until John the Baptist. I introduced him, you know. I told you what to look for when you saw him. He, in turn, introduced the Christ to the world. Now you have your Prophet, Priest, and King in one person, Jesus Christ the Righteous. Forget me if you like, but don't forget Him.